BEAT THE ODDS
in Business & Life

By Sandy Gennaro

With Steve Olivas

JRNYman Publishing, Nashville, TN

Testimonials

Sandy Gennaro is a true rock star on stage and in life. His history in music speaks for itself, but to last in that world, you must be a great businessman. In this book, Sandy will show you how to build and maintain relationships that are the bedrock of every business.

Scott Hamilton

Olympic Gold Medalist

I've known Sandy a long time. He is a great drummer and a good friend. He is all about helping people and being nice to them. I like that he uses many things he learned as a player in the music industry and has applied those concepts to real world business. Just because he is a nice guy, he gave me a phone number to call which led me to playing with Rod Stewart for seven years. Thanks, Sandy!

Carmine Appice

Fellow Musician and Drummer

Sandy Gennaro is a wonderful ambassador for hope, humility, and persistence. As a drummer that has performed with some of rock and roll's biggest acts, in some of the world's most renown venues, Sandy has never lost touch with the roots that grounded him during his early days in NYC. I am grateful that Sandy has taken the time to author Beat the Odds; it is a treasure, full of wisdom and inspiration.

Blain Wease

President–Provincial Development Group

I am so happy to have read Beat the Odds. Wow! I have learned that there are no shortcuts to long term success; you must fill your path with positive energy and good habits.

I have spent a lifetime in the hospitality industry, which includes 20 years with Harrah's and Caesar's entertainment and Churchill Downs. I have interacted with people who are dynamic celebrities: Gene Simmons and Paul Stanley of KISS, Willie Nelson, Paula Dean, Colin Powell, Tony Orlando, Paul McCartney, and Ahmad Rashad, to name a few. Although these people are impressive in their own right, none of them were as insightful, interesting, real, and inspirational as Sandy Gennaro. You will get to know and appreciate the upbeat attitude and positive energy of the author while reading his book. His real-life stories and suggestions acquired from more than 50 years on stage and in business will give you ideas applicable to your personal, professional, and/or spiritual life.

Two years ago, Sandy's stage acumen in Nashville opened the door to our friendship. His book established my interest in his mentorship going forward. His words are powerful, educational, and entertaining.

I share Sandy's passions for scuba, Yankees baseball, music, business, friends, God, and the joy of a good partner. Sandy has been blessed with a good life. He is grateful to God, his partner Shari, and everyone else who have assisted in defining his journey. I thank him for sharing his story.

Darold J. Londo

CEO/Executive/Entrepreneur

I have known Sandy for the past 35 years. During that time, I have come to know and admire him as a sincere, creative, hard-working individual. More than anything, Sandy is a person you always look forward to seeing. He radiates a positive energy that has made his speaking engagements as powerful as his performances with legendary rockers. He has created a new path as he ventures out from music to the rest of the world. His enthusiasm for sharing his journey inspires others looking for help, no matter what corner of the business world they inhabit. When positivity meets creative vision, you have the recipe for success.

You have Sandy Gennaro!

Rob Wallis

Founder–Hudson Music

This is one killer book! Personal, story-based, life-lessons abound for all who read it. In case you haven't realized it already, Sandy Gennaro is the Real Deal.

He and I have a lot in common: New York born, Italian heritage, Catholic faith, and a huge, loving family to die for. This has taught Sandy the important lessons in life–essential foundations that many business books today cannot begin to impart.

As Sandy suggests, grab your favorite imbibement, chill, and read one of the most enjoyable and valuable books of real business life!

Trust me, Sandy; you have made your dad proud!

Clark Vitulli

Founder/CEO/Board Chair–VISTAGE

C-Suite, Emerging Leaders, and SLT Group Facilitation and Coaching

After a concert, Sandy threw a drumstick to my handicapped wife, Angela. The next day, I messaged him to thank him, and I mentioned how much that meant to Angela. On a subsequent visit to Nashville for a speaking engagement, I sat down with Sandy and heard his David Wolfe Story. I knew right then he had a career ahead of him as a professional speaker. That story metaphorically speaks to so many listeners. It pertains to the "little people, little decisions, and little details" that are so easy to overlook and blow off. Ironically, when we take the "David Wolfes" in our lives seriously, their "little things" often lead to the biggest changes and outcomes, on and off the job. It may even change your life as it did with Sandy's!

I highly suggest you have Sandy Gennaro speak at an upcoming event that you or someone you know may be hosting. Sandy has been a professional musician for many decades, playing with some of the biggest names in music. The stories of how he created many of his opportunities are a gold mine of lessons for people in any business. Sandy's ability to tell the stories and connect the points of those stories to the real world is amazing. I highly endorse Sandy Gennaro!

"Antarctic" Mike Pierce

Professional Speaker & Storyteller

Published by JRNYman Publications, Nashville, TN

First edition.

Printed in the United States of America.

Edited by Allyson R. Brooks of Pandahead Productions.

Interior book design by Brett A. Brooks of Pandahead Productions.

Book cover design by Allyson R. Brooks of Pandahead Productions.

Cover photo of Sandy Gennaro by Ash Newel.

For more information, feel free to go to the author's website, www.sandygennaro.com.

Print ISBN: 9-781956-577020

Ebook ISBN: 9-781956-577037

This book is dedicated to the memory of
Peter Gennaro, Sadie Gennaro, and Jerry Athey.

Contents

Foreword

Vision. Foresight. Intuition. Instinct.

These are some of the adjectives that describe the greatest creators in history, from Steve Jobs to John Lennon to Ernest Hemingway. These extraordinary human beings seem to operate on a different plane, one step ahead of the rest of us. To watch these gifted people in action feels like a form of magic, inexplicable, and impossible to replicate. We have clumsy and incomplete explanations for their ethereal abilities. Media describe prodigies as having different brains, more neural pathways, and many genetic advantages. It gives the impression that greatness is bestowed at birth through a genetic lottery, while the rest of us are relegated to mediocrity.

Sandy Gennaro dispels that notion and demonstrates how greatness lies in each of us, and how an extraordinary life awaits if we follow a few simple life principles.

The circumstances of how I met Sandy underscore the lessons in his book. I am a former CEO, and I currently work as an Executive Coach. I have a blue-chip roster of coaching clients and I operate on a waitlist. Periodically, I organize retreats, bring my clients together, and hire a prominent speaker to energize the group and spur new ways of thinking. I meticulously plan these events and schedule speakers a year in advance. I put a lot of care and attention into these events because time is the most valuable commodity for my clients.

I was going over the details of an upcoming event when I got a call from the speaker, who informed me that he was sick and could not make the engagement. This revelation was two days before my event! I had twenty high-powered clients ready for a great day of leadership training, and I was suddenly without a keynote speaker. I was in a jam. How could I possibly find a suitable and compelling replacement speaker on such short notice?

I spent the day on the phone reaching out to my network, trying to secure a replacement speaker. I talked to a handful of prospective speakers, but either the timing didn't work, or they didn't convince me that they could carry a room of elite executives. Then, for some reason, I remember seeing a LinkedIn request from Sandy Gennaro a few weeks prior.

I don't typically accept LinkedIn requests from strangers. However, there was something about Sandy's outreach. He was friendly, unassuming, and his offer was simple: if I can ever be of assistance to you and your coaching practice, don't hesitate to reach out. Boom! I had a brief call with Sandy, and I explained the situation. I'm sure Sandy could hear the worry, bordering on panic, in my voice. He listened to me describe the problem and what I was looking for. He then calmly replied in his raspy, rock-n-roll voice, "Scott, I got you."

I must admit; before meeting Sandy, I was nervous. How in the world would a professional drummer with limited business and speaking experience deliver a meaningful presentation to a room of executives? It was a massive leap of faith. My credibility with my clients was on the line. Sandy showed up at the event with the humble, yet cool, swagger that only a musician of his stock can pull off. His message to the group started with a loud and raucous "Are you ready to rock?!" and then he spent the next several hours holding the room in the palm of his hand. Sandy told his life story of struggle and triumph, pain, and joy. He demonstrated how acts of greatness are attainable for all of us by following a few simple principles. For people with a positive mindset, who are committed to a vision, and who nurture and spread positive energy, the universe provides. Basic acts of humanity, respect for others, and kindness trigger Providence, where doors of opportunity begin to open in your favor.

Sandy's affable nature pours out on the pages of this book, offering insight into the success behind his rock-n-roll journey. I invite you to open your heart and your mind and get ready for doors to open!

Scott Morrow
CEO and Executive Coach

Acknowledgements

Special thanks to my God for all the good in my life.

Shari Gennaro and Jeri Gennaro
for their enduring love and inspiration.

Many thanks to:
Natalie & Mickey Williams
Paula Marino
Anne Marie Williams
Peter Marino
Dana Berman; Peter Williams
and Sue Athey Rink for the continuous love and support!

My sincere gratitude and appreciation to:
Joan Jett, Cyndi Lauper, Micky Dolenz, Carmine Appice,
Kenny & Meryl Laguna, Michael Pierce, Bob Moore, Gair Maxwell,
Clark Vitulli, Rod Thurley, Becky Sharpe, Tim Emmerich, Richard
Whitlock, Mark Tuchman, Charlie Wolf, Vistage International, and
Kevin Pokallus.

For all the millions of fans around the world that have moved to my
drumming over the years.
I do it for you!

And those who have been motivated by my Beat The Odds message:
You are my motivation!

Introduction

Too often, people expect the worst.

"I know that'll never happen."

"There's no way I could ever do that."

"Good things like that don't happen to people like me."

With that kind of expectation, it's no surprise! If you don't believe in good things and don't search for them—but you still expect them to materialize—you may keep yourself from ever finding anything. We can get so anxious worrying about the future; we lose the joy that comes with being eager. We also lose the ability to help ourselves when opportunity knocks. I firmly believe that sometimes an opportunity will come along in a person's life, but they don't see it because they're looking the other way.

I'm sure if you are a CEO, a business owner, or anyone who is just looking for some help, you may think, "Okay, Mr. Rock-n-Roll, why should I listen to you? All you do is bang on the drums all day. How could you possibly know how to help me?"

Okay. That's a fair question. I suggest you pour yourself a big cup of coffee (or whatever you drink while you read), kick back, and strap in. I'm ready if you are.

I'm not just from the music business; I'm from the world of business. I developed the Music Business program at The Collective in New York City, which has seen 25,000 students go through the program. From teaching, I moved to public speaking, becoming "The Rock and Roll Thought Leader." I've presented my methods to FedEx, Belmont University, Pacific Hotel Management, The School of Rock, and the U.S. Space and Rocket Center, to name a few. I've been a part of the world of business for over 50 years now.

So...who better to help you achieve rock star success than a guy who's been there?

***

Many books in the self-help genre give advice that's harmful at its worst, and useless at its best. Do this one simple trick, and you'll be rich/famous/perfect/good-looking/bullet-proof. The promises can be impossible and unrealistic (...*be just like Batman in five minutes!*). Very few self-help books are based on any kind of science. Others exist only as a marketing ploy to sell you more expensive books, seminars, and rocks from the author's backyard that will align your magnetic poles to bring you closer to your inner elitism.

I give ideas based in real-world common sense and basic psychology (I also give references to what I discuss). If you want to use my methods, you won't see results overnight; real change takes real work! And, if you are taking any medications and/or seeing a health professional, I will never tell you to stop! I want to help, not hurt!

***

During all my years in the music industry, I have developed a business acumen that I share with you throughout this book. I use my rock and roll stories as a practical way to show you how to incorporate these methods into your company, career, and life. Whether you are a CEO, an employee working for the CEO, or an individual who just wants to better themselves as a person, you'll find these ideas and strategies work on all levels. You will learn the methods that hall-of-fame rock stars use to create career longevity and trust among their employees, as well as maintain an ever-growing, multi-generational customer/fan base.

The stories of my career are the cornerstones of my business philosophy. They demonstrate how my philosophy of positivity, optimism, and saying yes lead to opportunity and growth. Positive energy naturally leads to better relationships. Better relationships lead to positive energy, and all the benefits that fall into place as a result.

You will have both the tools and the framework for knowing why. If you understand why you do certain things, you will have the mental flexibility to pivot and apply a different strategy if necessary. Without a broad, adaptable understanding, you'll end up dead in the water if your strategy doesn't work the first time.

All the events I talk about have depended upon certain altruistic concepts that I refer to as mindsets. As an example, I always treat others with respect. I do my best to help people when I can, even if there is no apparent benefit to me in the moment. I learned to say yes to opportunities. I know that through helping others and being good to all people, the universe will provide opportunities that will enhance my life and well-being.

I'm not advocating you make a wish and cross your fingers hoping it comes true. This book is about changing your approach to what you can and cannot control. I advocate an attitude that revolves around optimism, positivity, and personal connections to create the fuel in the engine that makes the world move forward.

My career was built on a series of unbelievable events falling at precisely the correct moments. Through it all, I have learned to trust whatever universal force guides us through the life we each lead. My journey provides all the evidence I need to believe there is a force greater than myself out there, watching over me and putting opportunity in my path.

You can take this ideology as a great sauce recipe, where ingredients blend into a delightful overall experience. Other methods are more of a simple fruit salad, where you could discard the grapes if you chose to. But when you take a bite of the fruit salad, you find the taste just doesn't work.

***

My hope in writing this book is for readers to begin looking ahead in their businesses and in their lives with positive anticipation.

I like for people to think about the future in the same way a kid thinks about Christmas. Remember back to a Christmas morning in your childhood. You would sneak downstairs ahead of your parents before they awakened (which I may have done a time or two myself in my youthful days). You would see the tree brightly decked out. Those glorious, glittering presents would be tucked underneath the tree, looking for the world like magical treasure chests filled with the fortunes and riches you dreamed of all year long.

That feeling in your heart—in the pit of your stomach—is no less than pure joy. It's a sensation of desire. You don't know what's in those presents, but you know it's going to be good. It could be a bicycle or a doll or a skateboard. Whatever it was, you couldn't wait to get your hands on the box and start tearing away the wrapping paper!

The future is like those wrapped presents. You don't know what lies ahead, but you know it's going to be good.

Real good.

PART 1: DOMINOS
Chapter 1: Changing Coasts

I began playing drums professionally in 1965. I was only 14 years old, performing in clubs and dances around New York City with cover bands. I wasn't old enough to drive, so I relied on my mother to schlep me and my gear to and from these early gigs. She was a trooper–she never uttered one complaint about being my chauffer. But without her support, I wouldn't have gotten off the ground. I owe my early success to her.

This was my life from 1965 until 1976.

In 1976, I married a woman I refer to as "my practice wife." It was my first marriage, and I was only 25 at that time. I apologize to all my readers for coming across like a jerk with that nickname. Even though we have long since divorced, I genuinely have great respect for her.

For our honeymoon, we took a trip to Los Angeles. While there, I ran into a wonderful old friend of mine from Staten Island named Frank Madeloni. As we re-connected, Frank planted a seed in my head. He suggested I move out of New York and move to Los Angeles.

So, why on earth should I listen to some guy from back home? Why should I pull up stakes and carry myself, my new wife, and all my belongings three to four thousand miles across the country? It's a crazy idea; what am I thinking?

First, Frank is no ordinary guy. He is a fellow musician. Frank is better known in the entertainment industry by his stage name: Earl Slick. He was David Bowie's guitar player from 1974 to 1976. He's worked with John Lennon, Yoko Ono, Robert Smith of The Cure, and The Stray Cats, among others. Frank's good—he knows music.

Also, during the mid 1970s, nearly all the clubs in New York were moving toward punk. The Ramones, Patti Smith, Richard Hell and the Voidoids, and other bands like them were taking over the New York music scene. The trend pushed a lot of rock clubs out of business, leaving those of us in rock and roll no place to be heard. That's why Frank suggested a move to Los Angeles.

To make his advice even harder to resist, Frank volunteered to help me out by introducing me around town. Also, both my wife and I had fallen in love with the beauty of this city. What started as a honeymoon ended up being a life-changing event. Thus, we took the plunge and moved across the country to The City of Angels.

On the plane bound for our new home, I made a promise to myself that I would never rely on cover bands for a living again. I made okay money playing cover songs, but that was all I got out of it. It put me in a rut while I watched my music career stagnate Understand that I find nothing wrong

My first apartment in L.A.

with the good folks who choose the cover band route—they keep great memories alive! But that path just wasn't for me. Even if I had to wait tables or work in a warehouse by day, I was determined to make it with a band that wrote their own music.

When we arrived in L.A., I got a day job at Wallichs Music City on Hollywood and Vine. It was the epicenter of the Los Angeles music scene. I was sure this would allow me to meet a lot of people by day and go out on auditions at night. Unfortunately, my plan didn't work. I went on a ton of auditions and played my heart out but didn't get a single offer.

Discouraged, I started to question whether I made a good decision to move to the West Coast. I couldn't "crack the code" of the L.A. musician's mentality. From my point of view, Los Angeles was a great place to be if you were part of a band that had already made it. If you were struggling to gain footing in the industry, it was brutal. I wasn't a part of the "clique." It felt like my big break was getting further and further away. Many people would tell me one thing, but then do another. So many times, I was told I would be a part of a band or a tour, only to never hear from the person again.

It was disheartening at best; at worst, it really ticked me off!

Despite all my frustration, I had almost forgotten one thing: when you feel surrounded by manure, don't forget to look for the flowers that grow in it. My friend, Frank, the man who encouraged me to go to L.A. in the first place, was the flower pushing my manure aside.

When I finally got settled into L.A., Frank threw a party for me, like any good friend would. He did it to get my feet wet in the music community, to meet important people, and begin to grow my network. It worked! There, I met Carmine Appice. Carmine was also a friend of Frank's. We got to know each other at the party and became good friends.

Carmine Appice was my drumming idol when I was a kid starting out in New York. His resume (if he even needs one) reads like a Who's Who of Rock and Roll. Carmine was the drummer in the band Vanilla Fudge. He went on to play with Cactus, Ozzy, Rod Stewart, and Jeff

Carmine Appice with me

Beck. Numerous drummers, such as Phil Collins, Neil Peart, John Bonham, and Ian Paice list him as a major musical influence. As for me, a regular fan, I found him inspiring.

Carmine was always very nice to me. If I saw him out and about, he always greeted me. When I attended his clinics, he'd take a moment to give me helpful advice. Afterwards, he always took the time to autograph whatever I brought with me.

Carmine Appice treated me with such kindness and respect that he made a lasting, positive impression on me. Inspired, I took his thoughtfulness to heart and made it a part of myself and my career. He was instrumental in creating the blazing arc of my career. This arc also involved dealing with adversity—something I desperately needed to learn.

With each domino that falls in one's life, a lesson is learned. Learn that lesson well, and a gift is given.

The next two dominos that fell changed my life.

Chapter 2: Dave in the Doorway

Inspired by Carmine's kindness, I created within myself a mindset based on belief, positive attitude, and service toward others. Naturally, this gave rise to opportunity.

Early on, my mother taught me to treat others with kindness and respect. With rare exception, I've lived my life that way. I firmly believe that if you treat others well—with no expectation of anything in return—you help yourself in the long run. I coach people to give to the world what they would like to have back. Take to heart a common saying: "Be the change you wish to see in the world." That mantra and that mindset have led to the most remarkable experiences I've ever had, both personally and professionally.

I remember times when a single moment changed the trajectory of my life. You have those moments, too. We all do. In that moment, you may encounter a person who compels you make a choice. Do you be kind and engage with this person, or do you lower your gaze and keep walking past them?

The mindset of kindness works on an uncomplicated level. A friendly "Good morning!" takes little time and effort on your behalf, but it may raise the spirit of the recipient. They, in turn, may brighten your day now that you've lifted them up within that one moment. They return the greeting, "Good morning!"

Now you both feel uplifted.

That small exchange would have never happened had you cast aside the opportunity to take the initiative. You made your life better by enhancing the life of someone else. Don't lose sight of the ripple impact—the continuation of your small effort. The person may share a "Good morning!" to two or three more people, spurred on by the good mood you created in them. The goodwill spreads from there.

Of course, not all encounters are that quick or easy. Some require a little more effort. Just like those presents under the tree on Christmas morning, you never know what your kindness can reveal.

You never know.

I had one powerful experience like that. The ripples it created grew into tidal waves.

***

13

It happened in the summer of 1981. I had moved back to New York and was hired to tour with the Pat Travers Band. We played a gig at the Hartford Civic Center in Connecticut in the dead of summer.

Pat was close to the peak of his popularity back then, touring to promote his newest album, Radio Active. The album Live! Go for What You Know had gone platinum, adding to the excitement of the tour. As a result, the arena was packed, and the air conditioning could barely keep up with all the hot-bodied humanity.

When we finished, we ran back to the dressing room and began celebrating another great show. We were soaked and exhausted, but high from the energy of the stage. Unfortunately, our tour manager harshed the buzz by pushing us to pack up and hit the road. We had a long drive ahead of us. The guys obliged, throwing their belongings into duffle bags and scurrying to the bus.

Being the sweaty drummer, I was typically the last guy out of the dressing room. As I gathered my personal belongings, the room became silent. However, I could hear echoes of laughter and shouts outside the door and down the hallway. It came from the roadies and union guys from the venue hard at work, striking the stage and preparing the building for whatever event was coming in tomorrow.

I paid it little heed. I was focused on my own process.

One thing I did notice was a guy who stood politely in the doorway of the dressing room. He had a small notepad, a pen, and a camera in his hands. I made eye contact and smiled while I rushed around and prepared to vacate.

I knew what the guy wanted. I had been on the road with big acts, and meeting the fans was expected after the show. I didn't know this guy personally, but he had a look I had seen a hundred times before— admiration and respect, with just a touch of fear. He didn't know exactly how to proceed, but he obviously wanted my autograph and a photo with me.

Here was a crossroad—a decision I had to make. There was never any doubt in my mind that I would engage this fellow. He was positioned right in the doorway, so I had to get past him one way or the other. As I saw it, I had three options:

1. Put the "rock star" hat on and completely blow him off. I might have smiled and nodded on my way out, or I might have just pushed my way past him and bolted.

2. Put the "polite rock star" hat on and give him a soft landing. On my way out, I might have said something like, "Hey buddy, I'm so sorry, but I don't have time right now. I have to get on the bus."

3. Make my mother proud and be kind to this patient guy.

The reality of the situation was that the principal entertainer, Pat Travers, was already on the bus with the rest of the guys. The fellow in the doorway was there to see me. For him, this encounter was so important that he was willing to stand and wait for me to do whatever it was I had to do before I left the dressing room.

His patience was a little humbling if I'm being honest. I've always welcomed the opportunity to put a smile on someone's face—big or small. I walked up to him and said, "Hey buddy...I'm really in a big hurry—but—what can I do for you?"

He lifted the pad of paper, "Would you mind signing this for me?"

I set down my bags. No matter how big the tour or the artist I'm working with is, I find these moments sincerely flattering. "I don't mind at all! What's your name?"

David "Dave in the Doorway" Wolff

"Dave." He eagerly handed me the pen.

I signed it and returned the pad to his hand. The tone of my body language implied I was rushed without seeming rude. "There you go, man." Just as I spun on my heels to beeline it to our bus, he made a second request.

"Could I take a picture with you?"

"Yeah, of course!"

He had a little Kodak Instamatic camera ready to shoot. When I leaned into him and smiled, he snapped the button immediately. Some people might think this was an inconvenience, but it only added five seconds to my departure. I grabbed my bag and hoisted it back over my shoulder. "Okay buddy, I gotta go. Anything else?"

Right on cue, he said, "Oh…just one more thing. I'm a bass player here in Connecticut. Would you recommend me for some gigs in New York City?"

Aside from being a little taken aback by his bravado, I obviously couldn't recommend him without hearing him play first. I told him this and pulled out my business card.

He accepted the card. Now it was his turn to be taken aback.

He looked down at the card, up at me, and then back down at the card. He acted as if I had just handed him a bar of gold. Wide-eyed, he said, "This…this is *your* home number and home address?"

"Yeah." This was back in the days before cell phones and instant access. I didn't have a business office or a personal manager at the time, so my card listed my personal contact information.

His next statement sounded like he was talking more to himself than to me.

"Sandy Gennaro is giving me his home number and his home address."

I jumped into his verbal thought and said, "No big deal, Dave. Just send me a cassette of you playing. That'll give me an idea of how you are as a player. I'll recommend you to some friends if you seem like a good fit. Then we'll see what happens."

He gave me a big hug. "Thank you so much!"

He kept thanking me and thanking me until I had to get the show on the road. No, really; everyone was waiting for me. "Dave, I gotta go!"

"Okay, okay…." He backed up a step so I could get out of the dressing room.

I got to the bus not knowing if I was ever going to hear from this gentleman again. But that didn't matter; I felt good seeing Dave respond the way he did.

16

A couple weeks later, a cassette showed up in the mail.

In all honesty, what I heard on the cassette wasn't all that good. Dave is still a friend to this day, so I don't mind saying that now. Still, I kept my promise and forwarded the tape to a couple friends in the music business. Nothing really came of it, but I made quite an impression on Dave.

After that, he'd call me roughly every few weeks. It was mostly just to chat, catch up, and find out how the other was doing. He was never a bother to me at all. If I had something to do or somewhere to be, he'd get off the phone without a fuss.

Throughout the next couple of years, we talked a couple dozen times. I never had an agenda and neither did he. We were just two musicians keeping in touch. I toured with Travers, and Dave made his way into artist management.

In the fall of 1983, during one of our normal calls, Dave says, "Hey Sandy, I want you to be the drummer in a band I represent."

I said, "What band is that?"

He said, "I just signed this girl to Epic Records. She's going to be the biggest star of 1984. I want you to be the drummer in her band."

I was a little worried I'd be overqualified for this gig, so I decided to let Dave down easy. "David, I can't join a baby band, man. I'm coming off an arena tour with Pat Travers."

Despite my protest, he persisted. "No Sandy, you don't understand. I don't want you to miss this opportunity. You were so nice to me in Hartford, and I love how you play drums. I think you would be a perfect fit for this band."

I tried to rub the concern out of my forehead and my temples. "C'mon Dave, I don't know." After all, I wasn't familiar with this artist's work or personality.

Still, he persisted. "Listen, Sandy, give it a chance. Come down to the studio and meet this girl. You'll see what I mean."

Dave himself had scouted her and signed her to manage. She had some regional success with a band called Blue Angel. But Dave found something extra in her that made him believe she was going to be a success to a much wider audience. After Dave pleaded his case on the phone, he sent me a tape with the bones of some of her songs. I liked what I heard. The young band had already laid down the basic tracks of their songs. The artist was now working on the overdubs, and it was time to hire a drummer to complete the project. After that, there'd be the usual album release and a tour. Work was already underway.

I made my way to The Record Plant, a prominent New York recording facility. There I met the artist, a four-year veteran of the New York touring scene named Cyndi Lauper.

When I first laid eyes on Cyndi, my immediate thought was when this woman gives an opinion, it must be heard. She was not subtle; she was not one to fly under the radar. She had a presence that demanded your attention.

I listened to her in the studio and was impressed by the material. Again, I liked what I heard. But I didn't give an immediate commitment–I wanted to take a breath before deciding. A day or two later, I called David to officially join the band. We met at a local deli to talk business, and I signed on.

I had previously toured with a band called Blackjack. And, as I mentioned, I had toured with Pat Travers. These had been very solid gigs. But the tour with Cyndi Lauper dwarfed anything I had ever done before. I ended up as a part of the rock 'n roll machinery that enables an artist to go from zero to six million over the course of six months. The album I heard in the studio was eventually titled She's So Unusual, and it sold over 6,000,000 copies worldwide.

David was spot-on with his assessment of her talent and her appeal.

My "Dave in the Doorway" was David Wolff, who became Cyndi Lauper's manager. He was a brilliant tactician when it came to marketing Cyndi early in her career. She had a confident vision. She wanted to dress her way, wear her hair her way, and make music her way. David protected and encouraged her vision, becoming a co-architect in building the brand that became a world-wide phenomenon.

Being good to Dave was the lead domino that tumbled into a global gig with Cyndi Lauper. But dominos aren't set up individually in a void—they are lined up to interact, to work as a group. The night with Dave in the Doorway was only the first of those dominos to fall.

***

At one point during the 1984 Cyndi Lauper tour, Joan Jett came to see her show. I wasn't aware she was there at the time; she mentioned it to me years later. As a matter of fact, Joan had attended two of Cyndi's shows. I doubt she was at the show looking for a drummer, but apparently, she was impressed enough with me that she offered me a job.

I honestly don't know if there's a direct correlation. Seeing me play with Lauper planted a seed in Joan's head. In 1989, when she needed a drummer to tour in support of her Up Your Alley album, I'm sure she had many drummers' names thrown at her. But she chose me.

Those beginning dominos fell in perfect synch.

An effortless show of goodwill to Dave led to playing in front of over a million fans all over the world on Cyndi's tour. That led to playing with Rock and Roll Hall of Famer Joan Jett. From her I learned the business of managing a band.

Quite the payback for befriending a stranger.

Getting paid well to tour the world and play songs that would be remembered by generations to come would be reward enough for signing an autograph and posing for a picture, right? Regardless, the best domino of all fell in between Cyndi and Joan.

At the risk of sounding like a bad infomercial at two in the morning...just wait! There's more!

***

Once Cyndi hit arena-level popularity, a large group of fans would mill around backstage for a meet and greet after the show. Cyndi made good use of this opportunity; she was a sharp industry insider who understood the value of treating her fans well. She was also naturally giving and energetic, so her marketing savvy perfectly matched her enthusiasm.

Shari and I in 1985

Since I was in the band, I'd participate in the party, too. I did my best to give the fans a positive experience that would bolster Cyndi's brand. Sure, I garnered thousands of fan interactions for myself over that year and a half. But I saw for myself the broad appeal of Cyndi, just like Dave had predicted years before.

On the last leg of the tour, we played the Charlotte Coliseum in North Carolina. I was doing my thing, chatting and posing for pictures, when I noticed two women sitting off to the side of the green room.

One of the two was very, very attractive. I made a mental note to meet that woman and introduce myself.

After the meet and greet, I approached her. I gestured to the chair next to her and asked, "Is there anybody sitting here?"

She didn't miss a beat, "Well, there is now."

Not wanting to be bested, I took the seat and fired back. "You're a regular Joan Rivers, aren't you?"

She smiled and introduced herself as Shari.

The floodgates opened to an enchanting conversation. After the show, she accompanied me back to the hotel and we had a drink. Not wanting the connection to end there, the next night she drove from Charlotte to Atlanta to our show there.

Shari and I in 2021

At the risk of sounding corny, it really was love at first sight for us. I sincerely mean that; we fell in love and haven't been apart from each other, physically or spiritually, since that epic night in Charlotte.

We maintained a long-distance relationship for all of 1984 and most of 1985. Shari came to New York for the first time on New Year's Eve of 1984-1985. The following November, she moved into my New York apartment with me. We married in 1990 and haven't looked back. She's my soulmate; my "other half of the sky," as John Lennon whispered to Yoko Ono at the beginning of his song, "Woman."

21

Being kind and engaging to Dave in the Doorway got me the gig of a lifetime–a tour behind a six-time platinum album. Out of that gig grew an opportunity to perform with Joan Jett, touring, recording, and learning from her. Best of all, the Dave in the Doorway domino ultimately led me to find my partner of 31 years and counting.

The mindset I will repeat several times throughout this book— be kind, be altruistic, say yes—is what keeps opening doors and providing opportunities. It is the force that makes the lead domino fall.

For most people, the events I've described would be enough to complete a career. But for me, Dave in the Doorway was only the first set of dominos. The second set led to major opportunities, both in terms of playing with headlining acts and keeping my cash flow stable for decades to come.

The lead domino in the second string fell when I uttered the word "Hello."

Chapter 3: Jerry Renino

In late 1986, I received a call from a complete stranger. It was a Wednesday afternoon, amid an awful winter. I was hunkered down in my warm New York apartment when the phone rang. "Hello?"

"Hi Sandy. My name is Jerry Renino. You don't know me from Adam, but I was given your name by [a mutual friend]. I was wondering if you could do me a big favor." I listened. He continued. "I've exhausted all other possibilities and I need a drummer for Saturday."

"What happened, Jerry?"

"I had a drummer, but he bailed on me. He can't do the gig." He outlined the details of what happened, then got to his point. "I need a drummer. I've tried a lot of other drummers, and nobody can do the gig on short notice, especially since this is a chart gig."

I sighed but didn't want to blow him off before I knew everything. "What gig is this, Jerry?"

He explained that he was the music director for an oldies band called The Tokens, whose biggest hit was "The Lion Sleeps Tonight." At this point in their evolution, they were known as Jay Siegel's Tokens. They were playing a show at the Westbury Music Fair, which was just a couple hours from my NYC apartment.

He offered to express ship a tape of the songs and the charts (music written out in a simplified way for a musician to learn quickly) to me if I agreed to help him out.

I knew the venue; I had played there with other bands before. "What does the gig pay?" It wasn't great. I closed my eyes, grimaced, and continued. "Are there drums there?"

"No," answered Jerry. "You've got to bring your own drums."

"What time is the gig?"

"Sound check is at three in the afternoon. There are four other oldies acts that same night, so we don't go on until nine o'clock."

The gig was at nine, but sound check was at three. I really didn't relish the thought of six long hours of downtime. I pressed Jerry for more information. "Well…what do we do in between?"

"We just hang around. But they will have dinner for us, so that's nice."

My hand tightened around the phone. Low pay, cheap catering, and a "hurry up and wait" schedule was less than ideal for any gig. Add to it I was looking at learning the charts, bringing my own drums, driving over 90 minutes in the dead of winter, and staying at a venue for well over six hours. Then, after the set is over, I would have to wait until the headlining act was finished before I could collect my drum kit from the stage. I would have to break down my drum kit and pack it back into my car. Then I drive over 90 minutes again, back home to Staten Island. This was the furthest thing from a desirable gig.

Yet, that little voice in my head told me do this gig. I truly wanted to help Jerry out. No one should be left in a lurch like this. He sounded sincere, and I knew what it was like to be over a barrel, hat in hand, as you asked someone for a hard favor.

I agreed to do it!

We played the gig, and I must admit, we had a really good time. Jay Siegel is a cool guy who I'm still in touch with to this day. He's the original lead voice in "The Lion Sleeps Tonight," and he still sings that iconic song in the same key as he did back in 1961 on the original recording. You couldn't mistake it for any other performance.

Jerry Renino and I also became good friends. He appreciated that I bailed him out of his jam. He's a good guy who established a good connection. And it was only the first domino in this fall.

The phone call from Jerry Renino was the gift that kept on giving.

***

It wasn't until the summer of 1987 that I learned how strong an impression I made on Jerry. I was still living in my apartment in New York when, once again, the phone rang. Of course, it was Jerry–but this time, his attitude had that Christmas gift excitement. "Hey Sandy! I'm now the musical director for The Monkees. Do you want to do that gig?"

He explained that the drummer they had lined up for the tour wasn't living up to expectations, so Jerry was charged with finding a replacement. Like The Token's gig, the Monkees were in the middle of a tour and Jerry needed the replacement immediately.

He sent me tapes of their live show. I made my own charts and learned their songs. The set list wasn't complicated, but I put in the work and arrived fully prepared to win the spot.

This was one of my favorite bands from childhood. I showed up to my first Monkees gig with the same excitement I had for them when I was a kid.

That opportunity didn't just keep me employed for that one single summer. I was also asked to do almost every single Monkees reunion tour and show from 1987 until 2012. During those years, I had the honor of performing in almost every solo show that Davy Jones and Mickey Dolenz did, as well.

Myself, Davy Jones, and Mickey Dolenz

25

After Davy passed in 2012, I didn't feel The Monkees could still truly be "The Monkees." Davy was such an integral part of their live performances, and it wasn't the same without him.

Despite this loss, the dominos were not to be denied. Jerry called, I kindly accepted The Tokens gig, which led to the Monkees 1987 tour, followed by several more Monkees tours, which seamlessly eased into touring with two individual members of the Monkees.

Each domino's click announced one opportunity after another.

***

As it goes with every "side man" musician, there is a challenge to maintaining a steady income. I really appreciated the tours Jerry sent me on, but that was not the only connection that stemmed from his call. Another string of dominos fell that helped keep my bills paid during those periods in between tours. This was enormous for me because I don't know what I would have done had the next series of events not happened.

As I mentioned, after getting off the phone with Jerry, he sent me tapes of the Monkees set list. I made my own charts from the charts he sent as well. Not a big deal; this was standard operational procedure. But I still had one problem.

Auditions require a lot of preparation and practice. I lived in a small apartment in New York at that time. Imagine being next to me, having to deal with a loud next-door neighbor who banged on his drums all night and all day. I didn't want to be "that guy," so I looked for rehearsal space nearby. I stumbled upon The Drummer's Collective, a music school that rented out rehearsal space. It's still around today; they've expanded the curriculum beyond percussion and shortened the name to The Collective.

I arrived at the location and went to the front desk to book a couple of hours. I entered the studio space, put on the headphones to listen to the tapes, and played along on drums. After my time expired, I went back to the front desk to pay. Nothing out of the ordinary for any customer.

But I'm not that ordinary.

Behind the counter stood Rob Wallace, one of the owners of The Drummer's Collective. As he took my check, he asked, "Hey Sandy, what were you doing in that room there?"

I explained that I was rehearsing for The Monkees tour. He seemed impressed, so he kept the conversation going. "Have you ever thought about teaching?"

"No...uh, no." In my mind, I thought, how in the world would I ever teach? I can barely read non-chart music. Heck, I've never taught anyone how to do anything, period!

Just as I let that thought settle into my head, my own wise mother's voice replaced it. If you want to learn how to swim, jump into the deep end of the pool. You'll learn how to swim fast.

Her words cleansed my soul of doubt and made me smile. She always knew how to give me courage. Bravely, I said to Rob, "You know what? I'll go ahead and try it."

Rob was delighted. "Great! I think you've got the right demeanor. You'll make a great teacher!" With that, we shook hands on it to seal the deal.

That handshake started my 27-year teaching career at The Collective in New York City.

***

Again, every touring musician—especially freelance musicians—must figure out a way to pay the bills when they are not on the road. If you're in a band selling millions of records worldwide, you've got steady money hitting your bank account, even when you're not on tour. Some musicians may get the opportunity to draw an actual salary as a hired employee of a band, so that provides them with a weekly paycheck, even when the band isn't touring.

As for me and most other freelance musicians, we struggle to keep the lights on. We may end up getting a non-musical day job to fill in the gaps between tours and album projects. We'll work a warehouse job, or fast food, or construction. Any work we can get and leave behind as fast as we find it works best.

The moment Rob and I shook hands, I had a new day job as a music instructor. Better still, I would get paid to teach my instrument! I had the skills. I had hundreds to thousands of hours of practice under my belt. I knew how to properly use a metronome. I could read and write charts. Now I could take my knowledge and share it with others by teaching the art of drumming to hundreds of students of all ages.

Soon, I found that the teacher became the student. I grew to be a much better drummer from teaching the drums. My sense of keeping time improved as the metronome's beat fell in sync with my own heartbeat. My ability to read charts became more fluent—I could quickly digest and master new material on the fly. I transformed into a skilled practitioner of percussion.

As my skills improved, so did my confidence. I accepted more complicated gigs that paid better. I felt comfortable in taking one-off gigs (shows where an artist needs a drummer for just one night), which increased both my earnings and my network tenfold. It was a relief to see my cash flow stabilize during the down times.

Working with The Collective was a stress-free process, too. When I went on the road, I would call them to black out the dates I was out of town  and unavailable to teach. When I returned home, they readily filled my calendar with eager students.

But the dominos didn't stop falling.

At The Collective, students were taught on multiple levels. They could take private, one-on-one lessons: one student worked with a single teacher who taught the mechanics and philosophy of drumming. The Collective also offered a 6-week intensive program, a one-year curriculum, and a two-year curriculum, all of which included music theory and technique.

I was teaching drums in just about every possible music genre. My students learned jazz, be-bop, reggae, big band. Whatever the students enjoyed and showed an aptitude in, I was there to instruct. However, what got me was the huge interest they had in the business side of music.

Graduating students were staying in New York to make their dreams come true by working hard and making money, so it made sense. At that time, no one taught business acumen to burgeoning rock stars. We've all read or heard stories of mega-artists getting ripped off by their managers, blowing through haystacks of cash, or getting in trouble with the IRS. The business end is extremely important at higher levels, but even the little guys working the trenches on weekends needed to know how to establish themselves as a business entity.

The students would ask relevant and meaningful questions, like:

How do I get an endorsement?

How much should I ask to get paid for (fill in the blank) tour?

I was offered a two-week tour. Who buys my drumsticks?

They needed answers, and I wanted to give them the benefit of my experience.

I went to John Castellano, the director of instruction at The Collective, and told him about all the questions from my students. We agreed the natural path to go was to create a curriculum that broke down the business side of the industry and arm students with the tools they needed away from the instrument.

John tasked me with creating a curriculum. Which, of course, I did.

I made two courses. One was for students who were going to be non-payroll employees, or "1099s." "1099" refers to the kind of tax form these folks get each year from their employer. They're put into different categories: freelancer, independent contractor, contractor, consultant, and gig worker (and yes, the IRS says each one is different). They are the hired guns who do studio work, go out with an artist on tour, or do a series of one-off gigs. In the United States, they're also responsible for paying income tax, Social Security, and Medicare all by themselves–an important thing for the students to learn!

The other course was for students who were "W-2s" (again, the name of the tax form used in the United States). They were the ones who join a band as a full-fledged employee on the band's payroll. The band, which is also incorporated as a business, pays the band member a salary and benefits. The corporate band will also take the taxes out of the member's salary to pay to the IRS. This curriculum taught the different considerations that the W-2s have from the 1099s.

The director of The Collective loved what I did. He immediately added the courses to the curriculum. Now, I was getting paid to provide private lessons and to conduct seminars on the business side of music once or twice per semester.

This is where my enjoyment of public speaking sprang from. Not only were the students at The Collective attending my seminars, but the staff hung flyers to encourage the public to attend for a small fee. I would be in front of a hundred people at some of these seminars. The experience and the regular practice honed my chops as a speaker.

In the early 1990s, my wife Shari and I began to seriously consider having a baby. I wasn't a starving musician by any means, but I knew a baby required more income than I was currently providing. We'd need a house, at the very least, along with many other ongoing expenses. I realized I needed to increase my income and save it.

I had no precise and careful plan formulated. But it seems that every time I have a need, the universe provides. I believe that God is my provider—it is up to you to name your own creator of providence. No matter the name, I have always found that something or someone in this big world has clearly looked out for me.

***

Yet another big benefit came from shaking John's hand: instructional videos.

I went to John Castellano to talk about an idea that had been on my mind. I noticed all the instructional drum videos at retail music stores such as Guitar Center or Sam Ash cost about thirty-five dollars. The videos showcased mainly hotshot drummers (well-known in the music industry as prominent studio/session drummers) like Steve Gaad, Simon Phillips, or Tommy Aldridge. These guys perform intricate solos in the video which tended to demoralize a young drummer, causing them to think, I could *never* do that!

I didn't want to risk turning off the next generation of potentially great drummers. I wanted to encourage and motivate them. My method was to stair-step the viewer, guiding them on a journey, instead of overwhelming them with fast hands and complicated beats. For me, the videos should be about the viewer's passion to learn, not the drummer's extraordinary abilities.

I discussed with John the need for a video that targets the basics of drumming. I envisioned a simple video starting at a ground-level. I described to him walking the beginner through the different parts of a drum set, describing each drum, and explaining its role in the overall sound effect.

Next, I would go through some very basic exercises to help the new drummer get a feel for the instrument. If a young kid or an inexperienced adult wanted to just try out drumming, they needed a video that could give them easy-to-understand instructions. Blasting beginners with advanced techniques and speed-demon riffs does nothing but frustrate the viewer. They need a plain-speaking guide to help them learn fundamental beats and navigation of the drum set itself.

John loved the idea! We decided that it would be best to break the forty five-minute video into two parts, especially if we wanted this for younger drummers. Each video presented the information in smaller bites, giving beginners an easier way to learn. It would also bring down the cost per video, thereby encouraging parents on a budget to buy it for their kids. The other forty-five-minute instructional tapes in music stores cost around $29.95 to $39.95 each. We decided to sell a Part I and Part II, thirty minutes per part, for $12.95 each.

To produce the videos, we went to video division of the Drummer's Collective called DCI. This arm of the company was headed by Rob Wallis and Paul Siegal. They used my specifications. We named the videos Drum Basics, with Sandy Gennaro, Step One and Two.

At some point while DCI was producing this work, Warner Brothers bought the distribution rights for videos produced by DCI. For me, this created more room for opportunity. Warner Brothers, being the wide-reaching media company they are, had the marketing team distribute the videos into retail outlets like Walmart and Target. Parents would have easier access to the videos; they could impulse-buy at the checkout counter or browse for them in the electronics section. No more special trips to specific, out-of-the-way music stores; our product was at hand and ready to take home while the family did their regular, everyday shopping. Warner Brother's distribution plan blew the top off sales and filled my coffers when I needed it most.

Most video contracts are structured like record contracts. The artist is given an advance from the media/music company. After the product recoups the advance through sales, the artist shares in the profits from that point forward. Sales were brisk for my videos, and I got a steady cut from the net profit.

One additional step initiated by Warner Brothers boosted sales of my videos even more. Warner Brothers had made a deal with Yamaha drums. With every set of Yamaha drums sold in the English-speaking world, my two-part instructional video series was included for a while. It was a great deal: buy a Yamaha drum set AND learn how to play it! It was as if you owned a tire company, and Ford Motor Company decided to put YOUR tires on every Ford sold. You'd get paid every time somebody purchased a Ford.

Now I was able to purchase the house Shari and I wanted on Staten Island, and we could raise our daughter responsibly and securely. I earned steady mailbox money at exactly the right time.

Was this windfall a coincidence? Not to me it wasn't. This was another example of a greater force looking out for me. I always felt that a big invisible hand guides me around this life, as if it were showing me a beautiful, golden path to follow. There is a grand plan; I just need to stop trying to force it. I trust that when I have a need, it will be fulfilled.

Let go. Let it be.

I don't know what steered me to toward The Drum Collective for my practice space in the first place. There were plenty of rehearsal rooms to rent in New York. Was it the price? Was it the location? Was it because they were listed alphabetically closest to the top of the category in the Yellow Pages? Were they the first ones to answer the phone when I called?

To be honest, I don't remember. But I'd like to believe it happened for a reason. It was part of a grand plan. Whichever universal force that has the big, invisible hand looked at me and said, "Sandy is a good guy; he helped Jerry Renino out of a jam. I'll guide him to The Drummer's Collective so he can have some good opportunities, too."

Good begets good. If you'd like to be looked upon as a good person, then be a good person. It may sound overly simplistic, but Mom's wisdom stands the test of time.

This all goes back to that first domino: saying yes to Jerry Renino for that Tokens show outside New York City in 1986. Playing all the shows with The Monkees, Davy Jones, and Micky Dolenz. Securing a day job teaching at The Drummer's Collective. Developing the Music Business curriculum. Developing my talent at public speaking. Making an instructional drum video series that sold like hotcakes. All of this happened because of one phone call and one word: YES.

Positivity; altruism; saying yes. Dominos click as they fall, and you unwrap the Christmas gift of your future.

***

I have one last story of how the universe provides.

I like to say, "If you want something, give something away." It's similar to Newton's third law of motion, the law of action and reaction (Editors of Encyclopaedia Britannica, 2021). For every action, there is a reaction—what I call the physics of life! Be a source of equilibrium for others and the boundless power and infinite wisdom of the universe will be the supplier of all good opportunities and inspiration.

This story will seem as improbable as an everyday guy from New York making it in the music industry and ending up performing in front of millions and millions of people over five decades. The way these events occurred is a testimony to how my higher power worked to bestow opportunity to me.

Shari and I were together for about five years before we got married. At that time, neither of us were in a particular hurry to get married. However, she began to drop hints about starting a family. I picked up on it quickly. As a drummer, I'm a very good listener.

Still, we got married. A few years afterward, Shari started dropping hints once again. She is not the type of woman to put pressure on me or enforce her will—her words were open and gentle. Thus, "starting a family" was the topic that entered our conversations again.

At first, I was on the fence. We had a perfect one-bedroom apartment, complete with a doorman, in the heart of Manhattan. I was touring, making a good living, and I was comfortable. Having a baby would mean moving—both literally and figuratively. We'd have to get a bigger place outside of the city, causing me to step out of my comfort zone. I would become a father as well as a husband and companion.

I decided to think on it. To give myself a little space to think, I got away for a few days on a scuba diving trip to Miami with my buddy, Peter "Mars" Cowling (may he rest in peace). I didn't know what to do, and I felt stuck within the decision. I prayed for a sign—and I believed I would get one.

I had known Peter for many years. He was the bass player for the Pat Travers Band when I worked with them. He and I had done many dives together; on this trip, we were eager to dive a tugboat wreck. Peter also knew that I was the type to snatch a souvenir from each trip. He warned me against taking anything alive—the coral itself was a critical part of the fragile coastal ecosystem.

No problem! I have respect for sea life, especially coral.

During the dive, I found an old brass porthole ring from the tugboat. It was green with mold and oxidation, but I "dusted" it off in the water and brought it back to our boat. Peter was impressed, and suggested I use a little Brasso on it to return its original shine. I was so

Mars Cowling and I

proud of the booty! I asked Peter if he knew the name of the tugboat. If I knew a little of the history, I could include it on whatever I did with the porthole ring.

He checked the dive manifest. "It's a Spanish tugboat called *La Concepcion*."

Or, as we'd say in English: The Conception.

I immediately perked up. I said to him, "Mars! You won't believe it! I came down here to think about whether or not Shari and I should have a baby. This is, like, a message from God."

How crazy of a coincidence was that? The universe reached down and pointed out a path for me. There was no way I could miss the message! God was taking care of me. It was that return of positive energy I had always talked about.

Preparing for a dive

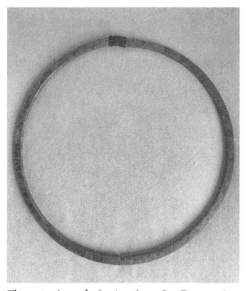

The actual porthole ring from La Concepcion

It helps to have a belief in a higher power—a universal force greater than yourself. I strongly believe in a common bond that unites all humanity and all the energy in the cosmos. That force controls the flow of energy and outcome. When you give goodwill, altruism, and positivity, it comes back to you. Keep your eyes open so you can spot opportunities to share your positivity. It can—and will—change your life.

As I sit here writing this, I am still as convinced today as I am of God's ability to make apples, that this was no coincidence. You never know when or how it works, but that higher power is constantly present. Sometimes, it urges you to scuba dive off the coast of Florida to discover a ship called La Concepcion. Some sort of entity planted

My daughter, Jeri, in 2021

opportunity in my path. Of all the places we could have dived, and of all the wrecks we could have explored, this is where we ended up on the exact weekend, I was mulling over the possibility of having a child.

It was all I needed. I went home and told Shari that we were going to have a baby, and that sent her to the moon. Within a few weeks she was pregnant.

We had our daughter, Jeri, on July 11, 1994.

She's the best gift God has ever given to me.

In hindsight, I'm glad the wreck wasn't named the "Contra-Ception!"

PART II: B-E-A-T-S
Chapter 4: Beating the Drums & Beating the Odds

I was told recently that acronyms are becoming passé in the speaking industry. But for me, they are a useful heuristic—a tool to help break down and comprehend complex concepts with an easy-to-digest word or phrase. I like to think about the steps toward action and change into one single word: BEATS. Each of these letters represents a universal principal that, if woven into the fabric of your everyday life, will encourage the universe to present opportunities to you. This idea works together with the falling dominos.

These principals create opportunities you may not have even thought were possible. They have the power to change your life.

B (Belief): Belief in a higher power, in yourself, in your goals, and in your company

E (Enthusiasm): Like a kid on Christmas morning, attack each day with an open mind

A (Attitude): The way you think, your mindset; the emotions that form your habits

T (Tenacity): Focus, despite the obstacles and naysayers encountered in your journey

S (Service): Altruism; doing for others without an expectation of reward

The way you think, your attitude, is the only thing you have total control over in your life. Our perception of events defines our reactions to them. The way you think is partly automatic and partly shaped by your intentional focus. It shapes your continued, evolving belief system and fuels your enthusiasm.

Altruism, for example, is the result of an attitude. You choose to focus outward instead of inward. In a similar way, beliefs are formed and reinforced by directed visualizations toward positive outcomes. Focusing on the positives and remaining optimistic will likewise create sustained enthusiasm. And finally, how much you are willing to put up with on your way to your goal—or tenacity—comes from the way you think. You prepare for adversity and deal with it as it arises rather than surrender to it.

All forward momentum and progress comes from your attitude—a mindset of positivity, optimism, and saying yes.

Therefore, I think of the BEATS hierarchy as looking like a pyramid:

Attitude

Enthusiasm   **Tenacity**

Belief   **Service**

With that in mind, each letter will be addressed in order, except for Attitude. Other chapters will address any subheadings within each letter, but Attitude is the flagship. Attitude is so foundational to the other letters. I believe it should go first. Each attribute relates to the other four letters because they require a positive mindset created by Attitude.

Chapter 5: Attitude

We all can think of someone who always seems to be in the right place at the right time. They always swim with the current and have the wind at their back. When they make a phone call, their message finds its way to the right person. It's not only in business that they operate this way—it's in every facet of their life.

So, how do they do that? What makes them different from you and me?

First, I must emphasize that the single most important factor is mindset. That person operates on a plane of positivity and service. Every company out there exists to make somebody's life better. The most successful people out there exist to do the same.

By "successful," I don't necessarily mean "financial." People who are truly centered and maintain a positive mindset can find success in every corner of their existence. They may not be wealthy but will be grateful for what they have. They may not have much but are happy to act with kindness and give to others. They always swim with the current because that's the only place they know where to swim!

In my estimation, we exist on this planet to help others. I encourage people to make everyone who has crossed their path better for having done so. They are setting the stage for a higher power to give back to them. This isn't about an organized religion or a particular philosophy. It's about recognizing something or someone on a plane above us humans who shows us that good begets good. It can be felt as an energy...a Supreme Energy!

The actions of that Energy are not immediate. The Energy isn't perfectly balanced. The Energy has its own pace and flow. I could not have predicted Dave Wolff would get me into Cyndi Lauper's band when I was kind to him. What I did wasn't about a reward for me—it was just my mindset of doing the right thing.

Pay attention to, and then self-edit, your thousands of daily little thoughts. Your little thoughts become bigger and bigger thoughts, especially after you dwell on their negativity and believe them. Over time, they determine your actions. Your actions determine your personality, your outcome in life, and how other people perceive you. Little negative thoughts are like mental cobwebs that grow and solidify into chain-link fences surrounding your life. They become your life, positively or negatively.

It's up to you whether or not to control those thoughts.

When somebody appears to have "the Midas Touch," where everything they try seems to work out perfectly, realize you are only seeing a part of the picture. As you read the Dave in the Doorway story, you may think, "Wow! Sandy nailed that one. He signed an autograph and got the Lauper gig," and leave it at that.

Here's what you miss: I was nice to a thousand Daves before I even met The Dave. Heck, it was more like ten thousand! My mindset didn't enable me to single out Dave Wolff so I could curry his favor and get him to sign me to a nice gig. That would be selfish and wrong. Instead, my mindset is one of service and gratitude. I am always flattered when someone wants my autograph, and I happily accommodate them. In my mind, they become my one single fan to serve.

If someone pointed out to me that one autograph launched my career with Cyndi Lauper, I would let that person know that their observation doesn't make sense. I don't believe that "luck" was everything, or that I was truly "blessed" to have stumbled blindly into that scenario. I don't think that way. Instead, I know that with every one of the 10,000 autographs I've signed over the years, I put more and more positive energy into the universe, so the rewards come back commensurate with the acts of selflessness and kindness.

I've done whatever I could for people and have reaped the benefit of humility and servitude. Think about it. Most people fiercely protect all they have, and eventually watch it dwindle over time. Instead, they could send a pulse of positive energy into the world and watch the benefit grow over time.

Be aware of your intentions. That universal higher power will sniff out an ulterior motive. It's hard to get away with being smarmy over the long haul. Plus, it will feed a mindset of negativity.

Let's look at a few hypothetical Dave-In-The-Doorway scenes.

Imagine that Dave was a VIP; a high roller who I thought I could benefit from down the road at another point in time. If I had chosen to be nice to Dave solely for self-serving reasons, what would happen? More than likely, Dave would tell that I only wanted something out of him for myself.

It could be that Dave is a genuinely kind-hearted guy. He's just so happy to have the autograph, he doesn't really mind that I want something out of him.

Or he could be selfish and self-centered, just like me. He'll use his "street cred" to get the autograph he wants out of me. As soon as he gets it, I'm history. I'm just another splotch of roadkill in his rear-view mirror.

Maybe he was with his cute sister at the show. I figure that, if I were friendly, I could get a date with Sis. After autographing his notepad and taking the picture, maybe he senses I'm coming onto his sister, and he finds that offensive. If I'm lucky, I may walk away with only a black eye.

Maybe, after the autograph and the picture, his *sister* senses my crude approach and she's the one giving me a black eye!

In these scenarios, I walk away hurt, frustrated, and resentful. I gave the guy what he asked for, but he gave me nothing I wanted in return. My thought becomes *screw that guy!*

Perhaps, a couple of days later, I'm playing somewhere in Arkansas. If I see a different guy standing in the doorway, waiting patiently to get my autograph, I'll remember what happened to me before and think, *screw that guy, too!* Why should I go through all the fan service when I'm just going to feel lousy afterward?

Good begets good; negativity begets negativity. What you give to the world automatically spreads out to the universe. Opportunities will open as a result if your intentions and actions are altruistic. You've got to keep your eyes open, keep believing in yourself and your positive mindset, and keep your visualizations of success alive and active. When you see an opportunity arise, take advantage of it. Reap the benefit of the universe providing for you.

I don't know specifically how this all works. Instead, what I can do is encourage you to try it.

Try it.

***

A positive attitude isn't an empty platitude. It is a genuine mindset that is within your control. You are the one who decides how you will read a situation and react to it. This is a fully realized concept that has some science behind it!

Martin Seligman is an American psychologist. He has worked as a Professor of Psychology at Cornell and the University of Pennsylvania, as well as serving as the President of the American Psychological Association in 1998. He is the founding editor-in-chief of the

41

Prevention and Treatment journal and is on the board of advisors for Parents magazine. He's also the father of Modern Positive Psychology (Hirtz, 1999).

Seligman is best known for his concept of "learned helplessness." Through his experiments, he found that when someone feels unable to escape bad situations, they'll ignore new opportunities to learn how to escape (Seligman, 1992).

Later, Seligman attended a conference at the MacArthur Foundation and met the world-renown polio vaccine scientist Dr. Jonas Salk. Salk told Seligman that he wished he could psychologically immunize children to help them fight mental illness (Hirtz, 1999). This talk changed Seligman's way of thinking—if people learned pessimism, then they could learn optimism! By combining theories of biochemistry, behaviorism, evolution, and genetics, he found that, even though there are some things about ourselves we can't control, we can learn happiness and optimism (Seligman, 1993).

You probably know people who, despite terrible events transpiring in their lives, always seem upbeat and look toward a brighter future. Conversely, I'm sure you've all been around people who can find the dark lining in any silver cloud. Through cognitive restructuring (reformatting the negative attitude files on your internal hard drive) we can essentially retrain our brain to approach life in a different way. The challenge is to recognize this tendency in ourselves and have the motivation to change it.

***

If you are the type of person who looks ahead to a brighter future, good for you! You have a mindset and emotional regulation system that will benefit your health—both mental and physical—for years to come. You will feel less overall frustration, hostility, and protracted grief than your peers. Keep up the good work!

Should you find yourself on the opposite end of the spectrum, however, use the following six principles to build and bolster your optimism.

First: Pay attention to how you talk, both externally (to other people) and internally (to yourself). Your thoughts are reinforced through repetition. If you experience an event, and then tell yourself repeatedly that this is the worst thing that could ever happen, that your recovery will be impossible, and that you will never be able to move on, you will create that exact outcome.

Further, if you mention these thoughts to other people, you exponentially reinforce that negative spin. You need to formulate the thought (one repetition), you have to translate the thought into words (second exposure/repetition), you have to speak the words out loud (third), you hear the words you are saying (fourth), and you experience the reaction—and possible collusion—of the person you are telling. That's five exposures, or repetitions, of that single negative thought. The reinforcement of that repeated cycle will invariably create a cocoon of Truth (with a capital "T") around the thought. Lather, rinse, repeat. You shape your mindset to accept the negative as Truth.

If a person with this mindset tries to change the way they think, they'll find it to be a challenge at first. Recognizing the problem is a critical first step. Most people who think in a negative manner will react to this example by saying, "Yeah, but what if all that negative stuff is true?" In that question lies both the obstacle and the solution.

These folks would be surprised to hear that opportunity lives within a crisis. A old saying that embodies this conviction is, "God closes a door, but opens a window." That's thinking optimistically. Bend the brain to think about possible outcomes that are productive rather than destructive. Action is required to overcome a problem. You could sit and mope at your "action of choice," or you could try something different…something new. It may fail, but even that failure will help you learn and create a new action that will take you closer to a better outcome.

Second: Take inventory of the positives. It may sound a little hokey but doing this can build a more positive mindset. People with a negative mindset can deny the existence of all positives in a situation. To them, finding a silver lining is an exercise in futility because they see nothing but a negative outcome. However, brain-storming the potential upsides of any event can not only create new solutions but shift the focus from the negative to the positive.

From a business standpoint, when a situation impacts a company negatively, it is up to the leadership team to keep employees motivated and creative. In the boardroom or on a conference call, managers can intentionally lead their employees to this path. Taking a moment to allow everyone to air complaints may be a productive use of time. It is good to allow employees a moment to express and release their pent-up anxiety. But right after sinking into the quicksand of stress, ease away from the negative chatter and ask employees what the possible upsides are to the issue at hand.

Having them hear that you, the leader, are not going to succumb to panic can be profound in allaying their fears. It will adjust the team's mindset to focus on solutions rather than despair. Additionally, someone around the table may see something in the problem—maybe a new twist or an avenue you hadn't seen—that can start the team toward completely reframing the problem into an opportunity.

Third: Fortify your relationships with people who share an optimistic point of view. When it comes to romance, friendships, and acquaintances, people tend to gravitate toward like-minded individuals. Think about the kind of person you tend to be attracted to. Here, I don't necessarily mean in a romantic or sexual way. I'm referring to friends and other people you like to hang around.

Of the two phrases "birds of a feather flock together" and "opposites attract," which holds truer for you? Research shows we have a lot more in common with birds than with magnets (Lazarsfeld & Merton, 1954). We tend to be drawn toward people who are like us. Those who share common interests and similar points of view in the way of politics, religion, finance, and other areas, are the most comfortable people for us to bond with.

Taking that concept and expanding upon it, consider this idiom: misery loves company. Do you believe that is true? Research shows that misery does love company—but only a certain kind of company (Schacter, 1959). Misery loves miserable company.

If you break it down, it makes sense. When we feel strongly about a concept or issue, we like to feel a sense of universality. We don't want to be the only one going through an experience. If we can find someone who vibes with our wavelength, we are immediately drawn to that person. As a species, we do enjoy commiserating.

As we put all these concepts together, we can inadvertently submerge ourselves into an echo chamber of negativity. We are attracted to people who think like us and share our angst, so we form a social huddle of like-minded folks who end up reinforcing and exacerbating the negativity in each other.

I'm sure you've all worked in a setting where one toxic coworker can surreptitiously bring together and ignite coworkers with toxic potential. Over time, that person's negative and subversive thought process can pervade the entire workforce. These become the employees the managers work diligently to redirect or eliminate.

If you find yourself surrounded by a negative social circle—whether at work, home, or social media—work intentionally to pull away and form a group with more positive people.

Of course, nobody likes the adult cheerleader who constantly sings about how everything is wonderful all the time. But the opposite is just as true. Nobody likes the energy-sucking vacuum of a human Eeyore who is always directing the conversation back to negative thoughts or perceptions.

Fourth: Be a positive leader. I always strongly coach managers to focus on positives when engaging with employees. Normally, managers lead their employees in a way consistent with what they believe motivates the employees. To be better managers, they must first take a hard, honest look how they manage and what they truly believe. Does the manager assume that employees hate their work and are only motivated by a paycheck? Or does the manager assume that employees really want to be involved and do a good job? An American management professor and researcher named Douglas McGregor labeled these two types of management styles as Theory X (externally motivated) and Theory Y (internally motivated), respectively (McGregor, 1960).

With Theory X, the employee's motivation comes from an external source: a manager, supervisor, or any other person in charge of that employee. If a manager believes that employees will perform poorly if they are not constantly kept in check using his or her influence, that manager will also spend an inordinate amount of time commenting on the employee's negatives or weaknesses (sometimes disguised by the buzzword "growth areas"). If the employees know that any time the manager wants to "have a dialogue" with them about their poor performance, the employee will feel continually stressed while they perpetually look over their shoulder (McGregor, 1960).

A better strategy to build a positive work force is to employ McGregor's method of Theory Y, wherein the manager sees the employee as an asset to the company and treat them as such. The employees are motivated because they feel their internal, intrinsic abilities are appreciated (1960).

My suggestion for positive management is akin something I call, "catch them being good." I borrowed this phrase from about a thousand parenting books, and I think it holds true all along the human experience.

In the workplace, because we are working with adults, we use a phrase that's more appropriate: "praise-positive performance." This avoids the authoritative dynamic of the parent/child relationship. Small affirmations throughout the day can boost morale, which leads to employees feeling more satisfied and less encumbered at work. This, in turn, yields higher productivity and creativity.

Simple verbal acknowledgements take almost no energy and even less time on behalf of the manager. It can have a positive ripple effect throughout the workforce. Plus, it can help mitigate the emotional impact of corrective feedback. The employee will enter a conversation with management knowing the assessment will be fair and balanced.

On a much wider scale, if anyone (an employee or coworker or child or spouse) knows the compliments they receive are genuine, then they trust their relationship with the person who gave them. The relationship grows because people react better to reward than punishment.

Fifth: Anchor yourself in the present. Psychologists often talk about the unhealthy practice of "living in the past" and "living in the future." Dwelling too much in one's past can lead to depression. Constantly looking ahead with worry can lead to anxiety. Not everyone does this in all situations, of course, but any activity done to this extreme does not promote a positive attitude.

When the people in the workplace are on edge, they are probably looking ahead to a dreadful, negative outcome. They rush to avoid the negative, which means they are over-focused on that negative. Some very rare instances of this behavior may require punitive action. But positive-minded managers coach employees to focus on the day and the task at hand. The employees feel secure within their workplace environment. Proactive, solution-focused thinking requires us to face reality on reality's terms, and we can create a flow of energy toward a positive outcome.

Sixth: Prepare for the unexpected. This is a concept that plays a big role in optimism versus pessimism, and it can seem a little contradictory at first. But it is essential to keep a positive mindset during challenging times.

Simply speaking, bumps can happen along the way. That's the best time to be adaptable and flexible. In this context, preparing for the unexpected means to keep a positive mindset even if things do not go exactly as planned. The outcome is not necessarily a failure—rather, it paves a new road toward learning and experiencing opportunities that may have been missed the first time around.

These six simple principles can give you the foundation you need to be the best positive person you can be.

***

One big, noticeable part of my attitude is my enthusiastic passion. I am a fan. I am such a devoted fan of my wife, Shari, and our daughter, Jeri. I can't get enough of them! These two gals are the champions of my heart!

I am also a huge baseball fan. Even more so, I am a fan of the greatest team in sports history, the New York Yankees. I wish I had the space to regale you with stories from my youth, listening to ball games on the radio, and feeling awestruck by Yankee Stadium as a holy shrine.

I also have my baseball heroes. Warren Spahn, a great major league pitcher of the Boston/Milwaukee Braves, was one of the most consistent, methodical, and winningest pitchers of the past century of major league baseball. He still holds the major league record for most wins by a left-handed pitcher, despite a relatively low number of strikeouts. His gift was to make hitters hit his pitch. One of my favorite quotes of his goes, "A pitcher needs two pitches: one they're looking for, and the one to cross them up…" (Sports Reference, 2021).

Warren Spahn was a master of control.

He once told a story about a tight game he pitched during the 1957 World Series Championship. As the old anecdote goes, it was the first game of the series, bottom of the ninth, and the score was 1-0 in favor of the Milwaukee Braves—but the Yankees had the bases loaded. Spahn had pitched a no-hitter so far in the game, and he was beginning to tire. The pitching coach, Charlie Root, figured it was time to visit the mound, so he called for a timeout.

Charlie was a fierce, no-nonsense competitor with a very gruff demeanor. He stomped part of the way up to the mound, only to stop when he got within earshot of Spahn. From there, he yelled, "Don't walk this guy!" Root returned to the dugout with no other instruction to his pitcher.

Again, Warren Spahn was one of the most accurate and confident pitchers that had ever donned a uniform. But that one single statement, barked out by a habitually surly pitching coach, was all it took to rattle

47

Warren's winning mindset. Who knows what Charlie was thinking at the time? Was Charlie annoyed that Warren was getting tired? Did Charlie say it in jest to Warren when he got to the mound? Was it intended to be a quip to make Warren chuckle and relax? If the latter was the case, it didn't work.

Now, Warren Spahn was shaken, obsessed with doing everything he can to NOT throw ball four. His mind kept repeating, "I have to throw strikes…I have to throw strikes…."

Poor Warren Spahn walked the guy.

Charlie Root was fired at the end of the 1957 season, despite the Milwaukee Braves winning the World Series over my beloved New York Yankees. His firing had nothing to do with that moment with Warren Spahn; the manager, Fred Haney, wanted to populate the coaching staff with his own hand-selected coaches (Wolf, n.d.).

Yet, I can't help but think that somewhere, back in the part of his mind that harbored all his self-doubt, Charlie wondered, "What would have happened that day if, maybe, I had said something different to Warren? If I had gone all the up to the mound and said what I did without yelling it out like that? Or, what if I didn't do anything at all, and just trusted the boy to do his job? Sure, we won. But what was I thinking was going to happen?"

Charlie went on to be a pitching coach with other teams. I'm hoping that he learned enough that day to become a more positive coach. Better still, the Yankees became New York's premiere baseball team. And that is the unbiased mindset of this Yankees fan!

This story has become an inspiration for me regarding my mindset on parenting. Have you ever watched how some parents interact with their young children? Do you observe any interactions similar to the interaction between Warren Spahn and Charlie Root?

For example, if a child were to wander close to an electrical outlet, get too curious, and start playing with it, the parent might be inclined to channel their inner Charlie Root and yell, "Don't touch that!" That little kiddo would recoil in fright for a moment. But from that point forward, there is a chance that every time the child noticed an electric outlet, their curiosity would perk up, and they may be tempted to touch it. The prevailing thought in the child's head may be, "I can't touch this scary thing…I don't know why, but I can't touch this scary thing…I wonder what does happen when I touch this scary thing…."

The electric outlet becomes more prevalent in their mind simply from being made more aware of it. This is certainly not the outcome that any parent would have wanted. Instead of starting a drumbeat that doesn't follow the tempo of positive parenting, choose a beat that deflects the interest by not making the outlet a big deal.

Try saying something akin to, "Leave it. Move away, please. If you touch it, you may get a shock and then we have to take you to the doctor."

I want to emphasize two parts of this statement. First, tell the child what you want them to *do* instead of what you want them to *not do*. Create a positive mindset and lay out positive expectations. Rather than throw together a quick, mindless response that the child could push against ("Don't touch that!"), communicate expectations in a clear, relationship-focused way.

Kids often encounter that Charlie Root-type of empty command, especially troubled kids. They hear what they shouldn't do all the time. "Stop that!" "Don't do that!" "Knock it off!" "Quit that!" "You can't...." "You shouldn't...." "You won't...." "You're not supposed to...." If the child dares to counter with, "Why?" they're often met with an old, meaningless platitude. "Do as I say, not as I do!"

Thankfully, today's modern parents and teachers are slowly learning the value of mentorship rather than harsh discipline to ensure long-term success. If the child is doing something dangerous, act swiftly! But shaping behavior takes time and patience. Remind and reinforce appropriate behavior instead of denouncing and punishing bad behavior that may not have even happened yet!

Children who seem troublesome end up getting reprimanded for mistakes the adult anticipates the kid might make. Imagine how that makes the child feel! They react as if they are "the bad kid," unworthy and incapable of smart decisions. They will further deduce that the rest of the world sees them that way, too. In more specific terms, they substantiate an opinion they learn of themselves conveyed by their parents or teachers.

***

The work environment can function in a similar manner to the dynamic of a family. Present are parents (managers) and siblings (coworkers), all with similar interactions that go along with those relationships. Just as parents mentor their children's attitudes toward their siblings, the training that employees and managers receive as they grow with the company has an impact on how they behave with one another.

Executives and managers, no matter where they may be in the company's organizational chart, are tasked with being good leaders. They must be firm but flexible, transparent, relationship-focused, and demonstrate both a positive mindset and positive expectations. Your own leadership style should produce an environment that allows maximum growth, productivity, and creativity. And, above all, these qualities should always be standard operational procedure.

However, forging a positive mindset isn't easy because of the interactive way relationships work. Managers and employees play off each other and affect each other. Leaders must remain mindful of the employees' needs, but also monitor how those needs affect them. Treat employees with good will, but make sure that good will is within the parameters of your company. In other words, the overall mindset can't be impacted to such a degree that goals and tasks are thrown completely off course.

My good friend, Jerry Renino, the musical director for The Monkees, had this same difficult job to do. He had to balance his relationships with three separate CEOs (Chief Executive Officers): Davy Jones, Micky Dolenz, and Peter Tork, just to do his job of COO (Chief Operating Officer). In other words, Jerry had to carry out the wishes of three different bosses, each with their own personalities, quirks, and egos, and still make sure the company stayed stable enough to make money.

Simple decisions, like song selection for the set list, order of songs on the set list, who says what during transitions, and so on had to be made by the artist and then carried out by the music director. In a show like The Monkees, all three of the main guys had been successful in their own right and on their own terms. Therefore, Jerry had to efficiently meld all their desires and demands when they were on stage together.

Jerry performed a monumental task.

Making one leader happy is achievable, especially if that artist is a relatively reasonable person. Despite many bizarre and famous stories, most artists reasonably understand the dynamics of live shows. Pressure, lack of sleep, control issues, and a host of other factors will come into play, but artists see their work for what it is. However, making three leaders happy—even if they're very understanding and easygoing—is challenging when the wants of one conflict with the needs of another.

I wouldn't wish Jerry's job on anyone, but he had the personality to make it work. He was the kind of guy who wanted everyone to like him, so he had no problem with most things the three Monkees asked of him. He kept the peace. He remained positive and made each of the three feel important and understood. He assured them that their needs would be taken care of. When one would have to be compromised in favor of another, Jerry did his best to balance the scales by communicating in an empathetic and positive manner.

It worked. He had the occasional rough time, but he got through it. As things progressed Jerry and I became very close; I loved him like a brother. I took it hard when he passed away a few years ago. He was a young man, but he made a lasting impression on my life.

Jerry Renino and I

I can completely relate to what Jerry faced as a musical director. When Bo Diddley and his band toured Europe, I was his musical director. It was my job to make sure everything related to on-stage content was exactly as Bo wanted it to be. From arrangements to intros and outros, to quirky parts of the show he liked to do, all of it was on me to convey to the band members and make it happen live.

I immensely respected Bo Diddley as a leader and as a human being. His expectations weren't complicated, so I enjoyed my role in his camp. From this experience, I learned that, like drummers, leaders should develop their technique; their "chops." A leader with "chops" knows when to be the frontman and when to let their employees in the band run with the beat. Bo was my CEO, and I was his COO; together, we were in sync.

Each member of the band had a unique personality and, as such, required different methods of encouragement and motivation. The group possessed unique personalities that, when combined, became a huge, different personality all on its own. I understood the interactions between each member, making me more effective in managing the group as a whole.

All the musicians with Bo were enormously creative. Often, they were like athletic dogs who needed to run every once in a while, to use their energy. But the mission of the band was to perform as a tight unit in the way the CEO wanted them to. Giving them a little leash at times and holding it close at others was my job as a good manager. I wasn't perfect by any means, but I developed a sense of when to do one or the other.

***

Genuine positive regard is the most powerful motivator.

When Joan Jett came off stage and said to me, "Sandy, man, you fucking rocked it tonight!" how do you think that made me feel? What would it have done for you?

Her enthusiastic statement had nothing to do with confirming my ego. She said it because she liked and valued my work, and that made me want to do even better for her.

Just as with parenting children, managing adults can achieve desired results when a system of rewards is used. One such powerful reward is recognition. Even the smallest words of encouragement will pump people up and make them proud to work for you or your company. When Joan Jett told me I "rocked it" that night, I was so proud I could have burst.

An employee who feels supported, encouraged, and praised for jobs well done by their boss will be far more likely to choose the high road when faced with an ambiguous or unsupervised moment. Obviously, this won't be true 100% of the time; we've all taken an occasional mental siesta at work! Yet, employees who internalize you as a good leader will want to perform in a way that makes you proud, or that supports your notion of them as a useful and valuable employee.

Of course, fear can motivate, too. Some believers of old-school management insist they can squeeze more work and more effort out of an employee by using strict discipline. They claim the fear of being reprimanded with the possibility of losing pay, or simply losing their job entirely, is what spurs employees into action.

One day, that same devalued employee may face a situation where the goal is not immediate, or the instructions may be vague. Perhaps the boss isn't around that afternoon, and the employee has a choice to make. Will they complete the task efficiently and to the best of their ability? Or will they decide that their unappreciated efforts are best put into something else instead of this project? Or this place of employment?

When browbeaten by a tyrannical boss, employees may relish an opportunity to put their thumb in the boss' eye, metaphorically speaking. They may feel completely justified tit for tat. This boss has never done anything but tear them down, so they sure as heck aren't going to go out of their way to help the boss or the company accomplish anything. They reflect the same contempt given to them.

If management continues with such a ham-fisted method, the company runs the risk of a high turnover. This leads to a reputation that makes it impossible to hire replacement employees. Once the hiring department finally does get potential candidates, the whole hiring process will cost the company a lot of lost time, lost productivity, and lost money, especially in the long run.

I'm sure every business owner, from Fortune 500 CEOs down to small business owners, can see the folly in negative-attitude management. Yet they don't want a workforce who are only there to punch the clock and go home. They want to invest in employees who take responsibility for their role in the overall vision of the company.

So, how do owners and managers receive genuine positive regard for the company when helping an hourly or salaried employee feel like they are a part of the company's success?

Those in charge must show employees that they are valued, not only as a key element in the company's vision, but as fellow human beings. If the employees feel they understand both the company's overall vision and their role in the company's mission, they will feel a sense of pride and responsibility in the company. Let the employees know they fit in!

Granted, a good leader can only be so transparent—confidential dealings must remain at the C level. But this information is such a small part of the whole picture that it (hopefully) becomes a moot point. Sometimes, information must be given on a need-to-know basis.

Executives and high-level management easily see their importance in the company. They are close to the top and probably have a financial stake (even if it's through a bonus structure) in how well they and their people perform. They grasp their fit within the success of the business.

Despite whatever title you may have, one truth is clear: *All people* within a company *are employees*. Executives (i.e., CEOs, CFOs, COOs, and other C-level people) are paid by the same company that mid-level managers, administrative assistants, engineers, coders, accountants, graphic designers, and others, are paid by. The only people who do not qualify as "employees" are shareholders and owners—they work only for a portion of the profits made by the company.

Thus, it should be no problem to talk to anyone in the company— they are all your co-workers! Treating them with equal respect is a important factor when letting them know how valued and important they are to the company as a whole. Showing them recognition and gratitude for their work only takes a few words and a few moments.

For instance:

"Hey, Pat! Your manager, Chris, told me that, thanks to your Marketing major, you came up with a great new idea to improve SEO! The people in Sales will be so happy to get more leads through the website, thanks to you. I am so glad you decided to intern with us. Way to go!"

This kind of support and encouragement is a part of the knowledge you already have. Knowledge of what's going on. Knowledge of your co-workers. Knowledge of what functions they actually perform for the company. When you communicate, be specific about what makes them valued and important. Your authentic effort is what will inspire everyone under the company's umbrella to do their very best.

Of course, managers who give only empty platitudes and generic praise inspire no one. Even worse are those who give only criticism. This is one of many reasons why employees left their jobs en masse in 2021, resulting in what was called The Great Resignation. Employees felt they were given no respect by the company they worked for. Bad management left employees with the feeling that they had no value and no importance (Parker & Horowitz, 2022).

Is this the leader you want to be?

I treat everyone the same, and I'd hope you would, too. Every person from the bottom to the top is critical. We all contribute a small flame to the big bonfire of humanity. In realizing this, we make all of us a lot stronger as we all pull together.

***

Creating and maintaining the strength of a good workplace relationship is primarily the responsibility of the manager—but employees can do their part to keep a good synergy flowing at work, too. You can keep a good employee by keeping a positive attitude at work.

As an example, I'm not the main attraction in any of the bands I play in. I don't write the songs, I don't step up front to wow everyone with a blazing guitar solo, and I'm not the singer who engages the audience as the face of the band. I'm just the guy who plays the drums. I don't say that to minimize the importance of my contribution. Rather, I want to stress how important it is to do a few things to help you prepare for opportunities that come along.

First and foremost, be good at what you do. Stay on top of your skills. For all I have accomplished, I still carve out the time to practice and rehearse. A lot of guys can play the drums, but I want to stand out as a proficient player. I want others to know that I'm committed to my craft and that I want to be the best drummer I can be. As an employee, keep in mind why someone would hire you instead of the person who interviews before or after you. What skill set can you bring to the table that makes you an invaluable "must hire?"

Pay attention to how you present yourself. I know the phrase "team player" gets overused in this world of corporate buzz-speak. However, working as a dedicated colleague can be what brings you respect from management and co-workers. This doesn't mean being a "yes man." Conversely, being argumentative or abrasive to the folks around you isn't helpful, either. Communicate. Take responsibility. Be flexible and reliable. Help willingly. Respect your team members. Take instruction. Embrace your role in the team. Working toward being a strong collaborator will make you and your company look good.

One tried-and-true business adage goes, "If a customer has a good experience, they'll tell one person. If they have a bad experience, they'll tell ten people." Don't kid yourself into thinking the world you work or live in is massive enough that your behavior will be kept in total isolation or anonymity. You develop your own reputation. Your reputation—good or bad—precedes you, and it can be what brings you the success you want.

As far as music goes, it takes twenty years to build a good reputation. It takes one bad night to kill it. It doesn't matter how good the reputation has been. If a musician shows up to a gig drunk, or fails to show up at all, they're history. Trust me; I've seen it happen. In my world, the network is small. Ironically, the longer a musician is in the business, the smaller their network becomes.

Being on the road and working with rock bands in the studio gives musicians ample time to interact and share stories from recording and touring. We're on stage with a headlining act for maybe an hour and a half, but we've got to live with each other on a bus for the other 22.5 hours. It's paramount that we can take direction and simply get along.

The people on any team know who is fun to work with and who is a pain in the neck. A musician's talent and ability on an instrument isn't the only indicator of whether they get the gig or not. A lot has to do with how they are as people. A lot of folks can play guitar out there. If I were to put a band together, who would I call? The player who is also a "good hang."

Be that person.

Last of all, be the one who says YES. In my situation, saying yes is imperative for survival, especially early on. I need to stay employed, so my reputation needs for me to be the guy who shows up when the call goes out. People remember those moments. If they are in a bind and a musician gives them the cold shoulder when they are in need, that musician falls off their mental Rolodex forever. But if they show up and bail the band out of a jam, they're now the first card in the Rolodex.

I get offers and get hired because the decision-makers (music directors, managers, artists) know they can count on me. Occasionally, I get burned and accept a job I shouldn't, but I still stick to my guns and insist on this: You never know. Pay attention to who is paying attention. Be a good employee and inspire the company to keep you for good!

***

Another facet of maintaining a positive attitude is attention to detail. If you are diligent, you will have a positive mindset. The two factors reinforce each other, creating a positive internal perspective. When you study the habits of successful people, you will find they are organized and attentive to details.

There are exceptions to this rule, of course. Albert Einstein was a notorious slob. Not only were his personal grooming habits suspect (he rarely wore socks or combed his hair), but his workspace was an unmitigated disaster. However, I suspect the details he was able to keep straight in his mind were razor sharp. Where would we be had Einstein not been precise in his calculations?

I encourage people to treat everything they do with the same respect and dignity for which they treat the people around them. Give the world the best version of you! Do those little things. Check the grammar and spelling of a text message or an email before hitting send. Make an impression that radiates competence. Develop habits that keep your mind and your business organized.

If you struggle with this, start with small steps to keep from getting overwhelmed. Incorporate small daily habits that are achievable. Vow to make your bed every morning. If dirty dishes get left on the counter, make the effort to put them in the dishwasher immediately after using them. Instead of leaving wet towels on the floor, or placing folded clothing on the dresser, or tossing your coat over the back of the recliner, decide to take the few immediate seconds or minutes it takes to complete the task.

Habits do not begin with one repetition; you must promise to yourself to complete the task every day for at least two weeks. Watch as you gain control over these easy, simple actions. The effort you make spills over into other aspects of your life.

Psychologists call these little tweaks to your life "Keystone Habits." Making the bed every day starts to change your internal impression of how well you are in control of your environment. Plus, you demonstrate for yourself how well you can complete a task. When you walk into your bedroom, it looks more organized.

You have now successfully achieved attention to that detail.

Change your mindset on these details. Don't settle with phrases like, "It's good enough," or "Nobody will notice," or "Whatever." Success is in the details. Make your version of what you do stand above everyone else because you took the time to make it great.

***

One attitude I think needs more attention is that amiable quality of having a friendly and pleasant manner: Likeability.

Why is likeability an important perception in this cut-throat world? It's because affable people inspire connection rather than divisiveness. And connection moves people forward.

The question is: How can you be highly productive and driven, but also be regarded favorably? It can be done! We have many examples of this around us. Perhaps one example can be seen in the world of sports.

Tom Brady is a great example of a "winner," especially when it comes to his success in American football. As of this writing, Tom is approaching 45 years of age and he is still playing the game (the average age of retirement for football players is 35)! He holds every major quarterback record. He's been to the Super Bowl ten times and won seven of those times. He's been the Super Bowl MVP five times and he's been selected to the Pro Bowl fifteen times. He is the only NFL quarterback named to two all-decade teams: the New England Patriots in the 2000s and the Tampa Bay Buccaneers in the 2010s. Most of all, he has never had a losing season! (Wessling, 2018)

But as hard as many people try, Tom Brady is a difficult man to hate because he is so likeable. One caveat here: I don't know the man personally. However, when I've seen him on television, he always treats people with kindness and respect. He chats amicably when interviewed by the media. He knows how polarizing politics can be, so he keeps his political leanings politely close to his vest. He helped a filmmaker make a football documentary by letting the filmmaker shoot his daily life for one season, on and off the field. He works hard to encourage good health for everyone, not just athletes, and he does so by quiet example rather than boisterous self-promotion. He uses his good sense of humor to absorb negativity thrown at him and turns it around with a smile and an air of dignity and self-respect.

Take a page from Tom Brady's playbook when coaching your employees. All the qualities of a good manager can trickle down to all employees if you act as a teacher and mentor as well as a manager. Attitudes such as patience and self-assuredness and reinforce them in employees when they are placed in situations that draw pressure from their peers.

***

I have a lot of stories regarding my career in the music industry, and I enjoy throwing in the occasional sports metaphor. But recently, somebody pointed out that some of my metaphors also involve nature. I do like to draw lessons from the simplicity and synchronicity of nature. I truly believe there is a powerful life energy in the Earth and in the universe. Tapping into this energy for personal renewal can help sustain the positive flow to your mindset.

I've seen that most people, at one point or another, struggle with frustration and burnout at home or at work. One therapy that works for me is getting out into nature and appreciating all that we see around us.

If I'm just generally in a bad mood—which happens to the best of us—I tell my dog, Angus, that we're going to the park. I wish I could enjoy anything as much as my dog loves going to the park. Seeing him light up and almost jump out of his skin with excitement helps to perk up my mood on even the worst of days. We get to the park, and it all gets better.

Being in the park and breathing in the fresh air is like a drug for me. I don't get high per se, but it calms the part of my mind that is fed up or annoyed. It turns my thoughts toward appreciation and positivity. I make it a point to focus on the things I am grateful for when I am out in nature. To me, it seems impossible to watch the sunrise or watch hawks circling the treetops and still feel pissed off that my car is taking an extra day to repair, or that the lawn guy ran over my sprinkler. Again.

Even bigger issues pale in comparison to the magnitude of nature's brilliance. If a big tour falls through (as happened to all of us musicians with COVID-19), or I miss a nice speaking gig, I can lose my perspective and my focus easily. But a trip with my dog to the nearby park helps to fit everything into perspective, no matter how bad I think it is.

We can have some control over where we steer our mind. As for me, it seems impossible for me to be in a grateful, appreciative mindset and still feel stressed or depressed. This may seem simplistic, but it is not possible to be grateful for what you do have yet be regretful or angry over what you do not have. It is one or the other. It is light or dark. They can't both exist in the same room.

Of course, the exception to this is the folks who do suffer from clinical depression. I would never want anyone to think I am belittling or shaming anyone who isn't neurotypical or who deal with mental health challenges. I support you, and I recognize the struggle you go through.

Nature is so enormous and gives us so much, I urge everyone to gain some perspective in life by getting out into nature and reprogramming your automatic thoughts toward positivity. Gratitude creates calm and motivates us to give back. If I say it once, I will say it a thousand times—good begets good. Take the initiative to bring joy to yourself and someone else today.

If you get that crazy joy that Angus gets when he grabs his tennis ball for a trip to the park, that's even better. Dogs teach us one great lesson: enjoy everything to the biggest level you can!

Chapter 6: Belief

Obviously, self-efficacy and confidence are required to begin any task. A strong sense of "belief in self" can also change your perception of what is possible beyond the immediate task. Cyndi Lauper is the exact personification of this perspective. If she could imagine it, she was certain she could somehow figure out a way to accomplish it. She liked those folks who would challenge the impossible. She surrounded herself with people who were eager to ask, "What needs to happen?" She made it easy for others to value her mindset of optimism.

But this didn't stop at belief in herself. She also had a strong belief in others.

We can believe in ourselves all we want, but many tasks in life require the assistance and expertise of others. We hire, associate, and work alongside people who have a variety of skill sets.

Cyndi Lauper knew what she wanted to accomplish on her albums and live stage shows. However, Cyndi couldn't play all the instruments. She had a solid working knowledge of music, but she needed skilled musicians who could join her in the pursuit of making her vision become reality. She told the musicians what to do instead of how to do it. She had a belief in us. The synchronicity of our talents and shared goals made wonderful music in the studio and on stage.

Sometimes, we have barriers placed between us and our goal. Believe in yourself and your goal can be a great tool to help overcome, then learn from the obstacle. You keep your eye on the prize. And believing in the people around you will elevate their motivation to not quit at the first sign of trouble. Perseverance begets success!

A leader's belief system influences those they lead. Your employees glean from their leaders' belief in themselves, in the company, and in their power to recognize and spot problems before they arise and escalate. Cyndi Lauper and Bo Diddley knew this. And so did a man behind a two-time, soft/pop rock hit single in the 1980s.

***

Cyndi Lauper

As a manager, David Wolff had clear goals for Cyndi. He wanted her to be the biggest touring act in the world, with the branding and merchandising tactics needed to drive record sales and concert attendance. His marketing plan made good use of her popularity.

He maneuvered her to appear in front of cameras and onto MTV. He lobbied hard to get her music a lot of expansive radio play. And he fashioned her fun look and effervescent attitude into a noteworthy brand. Cyndi's natural persona helped tremendously; she was eye-catchingly unique in the industry. Cyndi also had a voice range of four octaves, which few female rock singers at that time could boast of. Her look, a wildly eclectic visual definition of her joie de vivre, was unlike anything the industry and its consumers had ever seen before. Cyndi didn't manufacture anything about herself—none of her persona was fake or put-on. Her realness and her courage to show it were a perfect storm for a titanic branding strategy.

She and David took that shiny, spinning ball and ran with it, and no one could match their musical powerhouse. David boldly executed a strategy that paid off royally. He had an idea to cross-promote Cyndi to a radically different market. It required a leap of faith for a scheme that was unheard of in the music industry. His belief in Cyndi was what lead to the surprisingly successful outcome.

Cyndi Lauper's band, circa 1984

When Dave connected her brand to professional wrestling, he created an entirely new group of rabid loyal fans who wouldn't have given Cyndi a second look otherwise. Dave himself concocted the idea to match up Cyndi with the World Wrestling Federation/WWF (now World Wrestling Entertainment/WWE). He had always dreamed of bringing together his two favorite fandoms: rock music and wrestling. Now he had the perfect champions to pull it off. The storyline (or "angle," in wrestling parlance) involved Cyndi, Captain Lou Albano (who called her "Loopy Lauper" while he was still a "heel," or a bad guy), Rowdy Roddy Piper, Mr. T, "Cowboy" Bob Orton, Jr., and Hulk Hogan. It was billed as The Rock 'n' Wrestling Connection. The storyline reached its climax at the inaugural WrestleMania event on March 31, 1985 at Madison Square Garden.

Incidentally, Cyndi's band was briefed on the script beforehand by the WrestleMania production staff. We were to be in the audience when Dick Clark presented a platinum album award to Cyndi and Captain Lou. They had (in real life) raised over four million dollars for the Multiple Sclerosis Foundation, and the presentation at Madison Square Garden was the culminating event of their effort.

We were instructed that Roddy Piper would storm the ring with Bob Orton and snatch the award. Piper would throw Cyndi across the ring, smash the award over Dave Wolff's head, and finally exit while Hulk Hogan would rush in to help Cyndi. As a "badly injured" David Wolff would be wheeled out of the arena on a gurney, the band would leap to their feet, surround the stretcher, and act angry at the bad guys and concerned for their friend and manager, David.

I have to admit—getting the chance to be a part of something so crazy, so over-the-top was a heck of a lot of fun. I felt like I was a seven-year-old kid in the weirdest school play ever.

Of course, this market expansion of the Cyndi Lauper brand brought in more money. She was already beloved among her music fans, and she now had a throng of wrestling fans cheering for her, too. In the wrestling business, she was now a "face," a good guy. Because these new fans genuinely liked her, the sales of her music and merchandise grew by leaps and bounds.

The Rock 'n' Wrestling Connection also showed the world how fun Cyndi was. The music video for "Girls Just Wanna Have Fun" included Captain Lou Albano as her father. Lou was enormously popular at the time, so for him to endorse Cyndi and appear in her video was a great boost for her popularity. Thankfully, David Wolff's belief system kept him resolute and focused, even while his pro wrestling fan dream materialized right before his eyes.

And don't forget—even though David was instrumental in making Cyndi one of the biggest stars in the world, he never forgot the day I signed an autograph, posed for a photo, and took his phone calls at my house. A positive attitude, an optimistic mindset, and a powerful belief system. It works!

Bo Diddley

Bo was a wonderful person. I loved how he was always in tune with the world around him, and how he never lost his innocent fascination with the way nature worked. He had two farms, one in New Mexico back in the 1970s and one in Florida near Gainesville. He lived out the last 13 years of his life in the log cabin he built on the Florida farm. The land and the everyday townspeople around him kept him grounded and happy.

But his first love was always music. He believed in the business of music, too. He knew that by creating great music he'd encourage customers and employees to believe in his mission, thus fostering loyalty for his service and product. I know many people may have a hard time believing an old blues musician from Mississippi would have corporate-style business acumen, but he really did. And he did it his way—with common sense and plain language.

We were on tour in Europe, driving from gig to gig through the gorgeous rolling countryside. Somewhere in the middle of Germany, the driver had to pull the bus to the side of the road. The driver needed to rummage through one of the cargo bays for something, which gave Bo a chance to get out into the fresh air and tell a story.

Bo Diddley and I

Bo sat on the back steps of the bus and gazed out over a pond next to the road. When he spoke, it was to the bus driver. But he knew I was there, listening in on the whole tale.

On the pond was a momma duck, gliding along the water. Following her were a half dozen little ducklings, paddling as hard as they could to keep up with their mother. He gestured a gnarled, guitar-worn finger toward the ducks.

"You see those little ducks? They remind me. You know, when a little chick is born and his mother ain't around, so he sees your footsteps. He'll start following your footsteps around cuz he thinks you're his mamma. He'll follow you around, and he'll be walkin' with you forever because now he thinks you're his mamma."

Lucky for me, I was also recording this to video as I assumed a "fly on the wall" persona with my camera. And I'm so glad I did. This was a touching moment. It was an important story for Bo to tell— for him, the story was autobiographical.

Bo never really knew his birth mother. He was born in McComb, Mississippi to sixteen-year-old Ethel Wilson. Ethel was too young to raise a baby, so she asked her older cousin, Gussie McDaniel, to raise him. His birth name was Ellas Otha Bates. Following the adoption, Gussie moved him to the South Side of Chicago and changed his name to "Ellas McDaniel."

Bo related to the baby ducklings, which made his story immensely personal to him. His mother wasn't around, so he followed the steps of Gussie McDaniel. He always thought of Gussie as his mother, rarely giving his birth mother a second thought.

There is some science behind Bo's story, especially when it comes to fowl. What the baby ducks do (as well as all other baby fowl) is called filial imprinting, and it's a real thing (Lorenz, 1937). Many famous photographs of ethologist Konrad Lorenz show him walking around with a gaggle of graylag goose chicks waddling behind him. They had imprinted on him, and now treated him as their mother.

Filial imprinting is most evident in certain species of fowl, but the phenomenon can appear in other species. In fact, humans have this same instinct up to a point. And despite our evolved cerebral cortex, which gives us the power of rational thought, we are still controlled by parts of our primitive, lizard brain every so often (Keverne, 1996).

Believe it or not, this phenomenon can apply to certain business models and practices.

Performing with Bo in Amsterdam

The entire advertising industry spends billions of dollars trying to exploit this. Advertisements for products are, at a very basic level, trying to "imprint" their branding into the part of your brain, the hippocampus, that hangs on to memories. Through repetition (like creating television commercials you may see fifteen or twenty times) and sensory appeal (making the ad so visceral, you can almost smell the savory sausage pan pizza), an association is slowly cemented in your mind. Their goal is to train your brain to remember. The next time you're hungry—particularly the next time you're hungry for pizza— your brain remembers the pizza commercial you saw advertised during your favorite show.

Can you intellectually choose to order pizza from a different restaurant?

Sure!

Can you opt for a monster submarine sandwich instead?

Absolutely!

Those thoughts come from our advanced cerebral cortex right at the front of our head. Still, deep inside the good ol' hippocampus, will be this little tickle that says, "Hey! How about that delectable sausage pan pizza we saw?"

There's another part of the brain near the hippocampus called the amygdala, where we form strong emotions. That part will side with the hippocampus and say, "Oh, remember how much we love sausage on our pizza? Eating sausage pizza gives us the best feelings!"

The cerebral cortex, that big decision maker in our head, shrugs and gives in to the hippocampus and the amygdala. "Okay, fine. Let's get the pizza."

Thus, the connections are made. You now believe how good that pizza will be. You also believe in the pizza's ability to reduce the tension created by your hunger. That's the very simplified concept of imprinting and how marketing and advertising influence it.

Modern marketing and advertising demonstrate how brand loyalty is a form of imprinting used to maintain a long-term customer base. This is strongly evident in how a customer's experience can trigger connections like the ones that come from classical imprinting.

For example, if a customer feels engaged and important in your business, then they will associate your business with a warm feeling of acceptance and belonging. At my local grocery store, several of the employees know me by name. I always make it a point to check out their name badge, remember their name, and maybe have a brief conversation with them. Whether they are scanning and bagging my groceries or stocking the shelves as I wander past with my cart, I greet them by name. Through the years, some of the old timers recognize me and approach with a smile. We know a little about each other, and we'll take a moment or so to chat and catch up. We both have positive associations with each other, and we're happy about it.

There are other competing grocery stores in my little suburb of Nashville, and I have nothing against them. Some may have a better deal on chicken quarters or canned tuna; one may be a little closer to the place where I purchase gasoline. But I will still go to my favorite grocery store where I feel more like "one of the family," even if it's a little out of my way.

At first, I didn't notice right away that this was my thought process. But over time, it became clearer to me. I am now quite aware of the importance of connection in making a choice as simple as where to buy a gallon of milk.

When coaching your employees on customer engagement, emphasis making a connection to that customer. Ask their thoughts on the matter during the interview process. Connectivity is not about personality—it's about the willingness to engage and maintain a positive mindset. It's about reinforcing a belief in the product or service you sell and effective ways to show how your company will be the best thing for the customer.

I like to think of an 85/15 ratio when engaging a customer. During an encounter with either a new or established customer, about 85% of the conversation should be product-based. Whether you run a dry cleaner, an insurance agency, or a grocery store, customers are essentially at your business for a specific purpose. They are considering purchasing your product or service.

But keep 15% of the encounter set aside for more personal engagement. Listen for little hints the customer drops about a hobby ("I am looking for a good dado blade because I want to build a new birdhouse.") or a family member ("My son is getting into BMX racing, and he needs a good set of mud tires for his bike."), or their job ("My daughter and I are thinking about starting a food truck business, and want to ask you about the price of pork."). Each of those statements is a perfect lead into a business opportunity. Employees can guide the conversation into how the product or service will benefit the potential customer.

Employees with a natural curiosity about people will have an advantage if they can maintain the 85/15 rule. If the employee goes too deep into an engagement or a lopsided conversation (for instance, chatting 60% of the time about their own personal interests) can frustrate, creep out, or drive off a customer. But any employee can learn the art of maintaining and expanding a business conversation without awkwardness. After that, it's just a matter of committing certain information to memory.

All of us have the hard drive space in our brain to accomplish this type of customer experience. What's needed is positive motivation and mindset. Believe in your product and in yourself as an ambassador of the company. Believe in a positive outcome resulting from the relationships formed with your customer base. Your positive corporate mindset will foster employee loyalty, which will cascade into customer loyalty.

Work on forming positive connections with your employees and their feelings toward the company itself. This will result in a fresher, more positive mindset when employees arrive at work every day. If they feel they have a good relationship with their manager, they will be able to proactively problem solve before anything major goes wrong and feel comfortable working toward resolution if something does. They will believe in a positive outcome!

The best way to create this environment is to encourage managerial or ownership staff constantly model appropriate social skills, forward thinking, responsibility, and connection with their employees. The corporate culture will be one that creates and reinforces a pro-company and pro-customer mindset. You set the belief that positive expectations are the norm.

Just like Bo Diddley's ducklings, employees who feel connected to the company are more likely to stay employed with the company. High employee retention enhances your customers' experience; they see familiar faces, hear familiar voices over the phone, and recognize familiar names in email signatures when they engage your company. Familiarity breeds loyalty when the interaction with the familiar person is positive and uplifting.

A one-time customer is an acceptable benefit for some companies. However, a loyal, returning customer provides both a long-term revenue stream and solid word-of-mouth advertising for you around the community. A happy customer becomes the gift that keeps on giving. "Imprint" onto your employees who can then "imprint" onto your customers. A cycle of positivity and belief will perpetuate and sustain itself over time.

***

Into The Right Belief

Early in my career, I played in a band, Blackjack, which rehearsed at a studio in New York City. During a break one afternoon, I went into the hallway to feed a couple of quarters into the soda machine. As I contemplated my selection, I felt a tap on my shoulder. I turned to look at the tapper, but I didn't recognize him.

Thankfully, that didn't seem to bother him. "Was that you playing in that studio?" he asked.

I said, "Yeah. I'm the drummer. Our band is called Blackjack."

With no hesitation, he got right to the point. "Man, I'd really like you to play on my record."

I hesitated for just a moment, then explained that I just couldn't do that. I was already a member of a band—the same band I just mentioned five seconds earlier.

Without dismissing my concerns, he clarified his statement. "I'm not asking you to leave your band. I'm just asking if you'd play on my record. That's all."

"Hmm…." I stood, with those soda coins still in my hand, wondering what to do.

He seemed to understand my reluctance. He was in another studio not too far down the hall, so asked me to come listen to a few songs when I was finished the session with my band mates. That was fair, so I agreed.

The tune he played sounded up to snuff, so the idea of working with him interested me. I asked him his name. He thrust his hand out to shake mine and said, "Benny."

I had no idea who Benny was, and I certainly had no idea what kind of music he wrote. But I was moved by his appreciation of my own musical ability and how earnest he was when he approached me. I liked Benny's commitment to his work, and I could feel how strongly he believed in it.

As you know by now, I believe in myself and in the idea that the universe provides opportunities. So, I took a leap of faith—I decided to say yes.

As a courtesy to my bandmates in Blackjack, I talked with them about Benny's offer. They had no problem with me picking up a quick freelance gig, as long as it didn't interfere with our recording schedule. Everything was cool. I went back down the hall to tell Benny Mardones I was in.

He played a few more songs for me, one of which was "Into the Night." Just as before, I liked what I heard, and I happily contributed my talent to his album. However, I didn't take part in his tour; his offer was for just the recording work.

In the summer of 1980, "Into the Night" became a smash hit in several countries around the world. Benny's album—and that hit song specifically—became a major part of my resume going forward. Benny Mardones' song showed I had the chops to help create successful hit music.

"Into the Night" is one of only ten records to ever reach the top 20 on the Billboard Hot 100 chart twice. The original recording hit #11 in 1980, and then hit #20 when it was re-released in 1989.

As for the album I had rehearsed and recorded with Blackjack… it was a collection of solid and respectable tunes, but unfortunately it didn't sell or chart too well. But because I didn't totally jump ship for Mardones, I proved my integrity by honoring my obligation to my band and our work.

Chapter 7: Empowering Employees

When running a company, you don't have the power to be everywhere and do everything at every moment. Short of a solo, mom-and-pop organization, managing growth becomes one of the main challenges of a company. How to hire, how to delegate, and how to create clear job descriptions within the structural hierarchy are stressful tasks for leaders who manage the division of labor within a burgeoning business.

If you were a member of a company during its early stages (or if you started the company yourself), you were probably spread thin. The five year "rule of thumb" for a starting business tends to be accurate: The success or failure of a business can be determined after five years of operation. Those first years in the life a business are difficult. Gaining traction in the marketplace, evening out cash flow, training and retaining good employees, and just getting small tasks done, from filling out forms for a start-up loan to changing a burned-out light bulb, fledgling owners are always working, including nights and weekends.

After a few years in the trenches, that one person will take on the identity of the only one person who can do the job. You may find yourself chasing your tail, convinced that if you don't get the job done, it will never get done.

That thought is almost accurate. If somebody doesn't do the work, it will never get done. But you are not the only person who can cold-call a prospective client, who can balance the company's budget, or simply pick up a candy wrapper off the floor. It's easy to think about hiring a salesperson to handle the cold-calls or an accountant to keep the books, but what about that gum wrapper?

Obviously, you have to delegate specific business duties to your growing staff. Your office assistant answers the phones, your payroll accountant cuts the checks on payday, and so on. But what about all the things that fall through the cracks? What about problems that pop up from nowhere to give you headaches as they take up space in your already over-loaded schedule?

From picking up the candy wrapper to handling an upset customer, your staff has the ability to deal with things before they escalate to your desk. After all, if you purchase a defective product from Microsoft, do you demand to speak directly to Bill Gates?

Of course, you can—in a fantasy business world. In reality, Bill Gates will never hear your complaint. Microsoft has an entire network of employees who are equipped to handle concerns in a way that de-escalate and resolve the issue. Your company may not be the megalith that Microsoft is, but the concept remains the same. Training employees to spot, analyze, and respond to problems in real time propels a business forward instead of stagnating it.

I believe that entrepreneurs are wired to see problems, sometimes before they materialize, and work toward an immediate resolution. At first glance, this can seem like nitpicking and perfectionist. However, most business leaders who do this refer to themselves as "solution-oriented." Solution-oriented can turn a negative (the problem) into a positive (the solution).

I like to call this behavior a "habit of organization."

If I see a wrapper on the floor of my own home, I pick it up right then and toss it into the garbage can. I don't step over it because I didn't drop it there. I don't call my wife over, point to the wrapper on the floor, lecture her on how responsible people place their discarded wrappers into the garbage, or yell to everyone in the house, "WHO LEFT THEIR WRAPPER ON THE FLOOR!?"

Why spend the extra energy on what will ultimately be an exercise in futility? The person who dropped the wrapper may not realize they did so to begin with. Instead of going on a hunt for the guilty party, I bend over, pick up the wrapper, and toss it in the garbage, all in one fluid action. Problem solved. Move on.

As the head of my household, I recognize how important the details are. I am responsible for the cleanliness and overall functionality of my home. And I share this responsibility with my family. We understand the mission statement of The Gennaro Corporation: "All for one, and one for all." Success requires the contribution of everyone working together.

I could have been divisive and shaming with the candy wrapper. Or I could trust that if (heaven forbid) I'm the one who drops a candy wrapper, another member of Team Gennaro will sweep by and grab it on my behalf.

How did we arrive at a unified mindset? Reminding, teaching, and reinforcing behavior that lends itself to a sense of personal connection to the larger whole. Shari and I have had that mindset from day one. We are the CEOs of this business, after all.

But we must remember that nobody is born with problem-solving knowledge. This is where empowerment comes into play.

Hopefully, our parents instructed us on appropriate decision-making, modeled good behavior by their own actions, and reinforced the heck out of the moments when we did good work and participated as a great teammate. Shaping behavior for long-run success is the key to positive parenting. No mentoring parent would assume that a child should just know what to do.

Behavioral psychologists call this "shaping through successive approximations" (Skinner, 1953). This method reinforces the baby steps needed on the path to mastering more complex behavior. A savvy manager who shapes an employee's behavior has the wherewithal to patiently reinforce company-oriented beliefs and behavior, shaping a regular employee into a model employee.

Scolding, shaming, lecturing, and other punitive measures are inefficient tools used by unsuccessful bosses who unwittingly work against their own best interests. Shape behavior by reinforcing the good and not supporting the bad. Here are but a few ways to connect the employee to the concept of helping the company succeed by taking care of issues that cross their radar screen.

Focus on the overall purpose of their job rather than their specific tasks. Obviously, your employees will need to be educated on the different tasks they complete as a part of their job. Understanding the reason (the why behind the what) that employee is working for you can help them understand the way they fit into the company as a whole. Also, this helps to give the employee an understanding of how important their role—regardless of how small—is to the broader picture. How they perform is a critical cog in the company wheel that employs them, along with many other employees. In turn, the business may also be an important part of the community. If the employee can see how they are important to their managers and the CEO—and how they are thereby valued as an employee—they are more likely to develop personal responsibility in doing their job and be less prone to burnout or frustration.

Model appropriate behavior. When an employee approaches you with a problem, walk them through the steps of identifying how they could resolve the problem in this instance, then how they can manage it if it ever pops up again. Give them the tools of success.

Some problems lie outside the scope of the employee's ability. When this happens, you as a manager/executive/owner must act swiftly and decisively. Passing the buck, tossing responsibility back onto the employee, or delaying resolution will frustrate the employee, confound the problem by extending it, and show them that management isn't as dedicated to problem resolution as they claim to be. Show them their manager has their back. They learn from observing you!

Remain confident and supportive. I cannot stress the importance of managing through positive feedback rather than negative feedback. Some managers express concerns that, if they don't punish or micromanage, then nothing will get done. They have learned to only be Theory X managers.

Punishing your employee may stop tardiness, absenteeism, or sub-par work performance. But this is barely effective, even in the short-term. Encouraging the "all for one and one for all" mentality is always a better method for both short- and long-term work performance. Making workers feel as if they are sinners in the hands of an angry God (to quote Jonathan Edwards) will stifle creativity and kill off motivation.

If you're not familiar with Edwards, I suggest another old bit of wisdom: You'll catch more flies with honey than with vinegar.

Chapter 8: Enthusiasm

We all have lives that include time both in and out of the workplace. As a result, we open ourselves up to the natural ebb and flow of our general existence. Cars get flat tires, kids get sick, and spouses get cranky. At work, we have deadlines, errors, and duties.

How do we keep our enthusiasm in the face of all these adversities?

Every once in a while, take a step back and remember why you work so hard to attain your goals. Maybe you wanted to learn French because of a fun trip you're taking next summer. Maybe you need to complete a big project at work because it may lead to a promotion you've been eyeing. Maybe the same project must get done because you like your job! Maybe you need to rush home to get your kid to soccer practice because your kid really enjoys soccer, and it feels good to see your kid have so much fun.

Whatever the case and the context, you set goals because they make your life better. Reaching back and rekindling that motivational flame can help you keep your enthusiasm. Reminding yourself of the bigger picture can make seemingly insurmountable hurdles appear much more manageable.

Also, doing things that make other people happy will flow back to you and keep your enthusiasm high. Your kids, your spouse, your manager all tend to reflect good back toward good. Occasionally, you'll run into a classic sourpuss, but by and large, people are drawn toward enthusiastic and positive people. They reflect that positivity back to the giver, creating a beautifully infinite loop.

Enthusiasm does require energy, but it can provide energy to the people you rely on to help you out. Cyndi Lauper had some bad days like everyone else, but far and away, her normal demeanor was positive and her enthusiasm contagious.

Speaking as a musician and entertainer, an enthusiastic crowd gives me energy and makes me feel great. When a crowd is dancing, singing, and jumping around cheering, it's an injection of adrenaline to me. In turn, I want to make them happy. I try to push them to another level, just to see how much energy we can create together.

Acts of kindness and altruism create positive relationships. Positive relationships reflect positivity and create energy. Energy gives us the push we need to continue doing random acts of kindness and altruism, which help us overcome problems.

It's a beautiful circle of positivity, and one in which you control the key variable in the equation—YOU!

***

Talk of enthusiasm is meaningless without my favorite example: Cyndi Lauper is dynamic to her core! Her energy and playful exuberance for living life to the fullest is captivating and contagious. In my mind, she is the very personification of enthusiasm.

Back in 1984, I and the rest of her band had just played a concert at the Birmingham-Jefferson Convention Complex (BJCC, now called "Legacy Arena"), a 19,000-seat venue that was sold out. It was Halloween Eve, and Cyndi was at the peak of her popularity.

After the show, the band went out to a local club—and Cyndi joined us. Unlike other times when the manager would maybe call ahead and have the club prepare for our arrival, we went rogue and showed up unannounced.

A modest line of patrons waited to enter the club. We waited at the end, just like anyone else would. Cyndi was nothing if not humble— and she was always up for a good prank!

When we finally got in, we saw the club was hosting a costume contest. Cyndi caught wind of it, and turned to the rest of us, wild-eyed and mischievous.

"Watch this!"

She entered the costume contest. And she managed to pass herself off as an ordinary girl in a Cyndi Lauper costume.

On any other night, she could have gotten away with it. But not this night. Not right after the entire city rocked out to her music three blocks away, only a few hours earlier. The crowd was primed, and they knew exactly who Cyndi Lauper was, despite her ruse.

The crowd went nuts. She played it up, savoring the moment. It was pure joy to watch Cyndi having fun.

She genuinely liked hanging out with us. She is a people person and she draws energy from the positivity generated by everyone around her. With us, she was lively, thriving on the camaraderie of the band.

***

Cyndi is a testimony to how a single, thoughtful spark can bring together two worlds and create a magic moment.

When I was on tour with Davy Jones in 2004 to 2005. In between Monkees tours, Davy Jones and Mickey Dolenz would do solo tours, respectively, and many of us from the Monkees band traveled to perform with them. Davy was booked to play at the Texas State Fair in Dallas, Texas. The gig was on a Friday, so we all arrived the Thursday night before.

Friday morning, I got a call in my hotel room. It was Davy. "Hey Sandy! There's a guy down here in the lobby who says he knows you. He claims he's the drummer in Cyndi Lauper's band."

I blinked, a little confused. "What's his name?"

"His name is Sammy."

I laughed out loud—of course I knew this guy! Sammy Merendino! He was a good friend and an awesome touring drummer. I happily raced down to the lobby and nearly tackled Sammy with a big, friendly hug. I stepped back and asked the obvious question. "What are you doing in town?"

He replied, "We're playing the Texas State Fair tomorrow night."

This was cool news! I knew Cyndi was a big Davy Jones fan. And I knew that Davy was a big Cyndi Lauper fan. The gears in my mind started turning as I concocted a scheme to bring them together. I got Cyndi's hotel information and gave her a call. We chatted a little to catch up, then I put my plan in motion. In an off-hand manner, I oh-so-casually mentioned, "Hey Cyndi, we're playing the same gig tonight that you're playing tomorrow—the Texas State Fair! I'm touring with Davy Jones."

The excitement in her voice tore through the phone line. "Davy Jones? Of the Monkees?!"

"Yeah, yeah...."

"Sandy, I have this crazy Davy Jones fan story I tell at all my shows! It's about us walking along the beach and I have stars in my eyes!"

I laughed. Her imagination was as big as her enthusiasm. Still acting nonchalant, I continued to encourage her. "Cyndi, why don't you come down to the show?"

Although she could barely contain her excitement, she told me she'd see what she could do.

A tiny part of me wondered if she'd actually show up. After all, she is a very busy woman. If she didn't show, I'd totally understand. But I didn't lose hope. At the sound check that afternoon, I pulled the sound guy aside.

"Hey, listen…we may have a special guest at the show tonight. Could you do me a solid, and have a wireless mic ready to go, just in case?"

He gave me a knowing smile and a confident nod.

That night, the show went on as planned. It was a raucous crowd on a crazy-hot Texas night. We were performing as well as we always did when I glanced stage left. Just off-stage stood Cyndi, her violin player, and her road manager. I knew it! I lit up! I could see Cyndi, her head bobbing up and down in time to the music as she enjoyed the show.

This is going to be perfect.

Finally, we reached the end of the show. Our last song of the set was always "Daydream Believer." That was where my plan came together. And man, I love it when a plan comes together!

Myself, Cyndi Lauper, and Davy Jones

During the piano intro, the keyboard player hung on the intro riff while Davy told a quick story of his own. It would vary from show to show, depending upon his mood and his read of the crowd on that night.

As the piano played, Davy faced the audience. I stole the opportunity to sneak off stage left. In one motion, I handed Cyndi the microphone and gave her a quick kiss on the cheek. I led her out, my elbow hooked around hers, and tapped Davy on the shoulder.

He turned around and lit up like truckload of Roman candles on the Fourth of July! He grabbed Cyndi's hand and dragged her stage front. With a fanboy gush in his voice, he introduced her to the crowd. "Oh, man! Ladies and gentlemen! Cyndi Lauper!"

The crowd went crazy!

The two of them sang "Daydream Believer" together. It was completely unrehearsed, and they nailed it like the pros they are. Cyndi knew all the words, and she instinctively knew how to play off Davy like they had been performing the song for years.

It was such an awesome moment, and I was so glad I could make it happen for both.

***

If you can't tell by now, I have a tremendous amount of respect for Cyndi Lauper. Because of her, so many wondrous things have happened to me and my career.

Yet, for all the praise I heap onto Cyndi, I also have an equally massive amount of respect for Joan Jett. They are two very different women, but both have star qualities, are consummate professionals, and carry themselves with dignity, confidence, and grace.

The difference? Cyndi showed me the importance of enthusiasm. Joan taught me how to be a good manager.

The most influential person in my career was a producer named Tom Dowd, who will always represent the pinnacle of leadership for me. But Joan was a very, very close second.

In 1989, I went on tour with Joan Jett as her drummer during her Up Your Alley tour. Joan was an established star long before I entered her camp. She knew how to handle the pressure of being a feature performer and how to effectively manage her people.

She knew full well she oversaw her "Blackheart Corporation." As the CEO, she had to get things done for her customers—the fans. She made sure her employees—her band mates—were happy and stable. She made sure to keep money flowing that fed the machinery which kept us all employed and on the road.

79

While on the road, Joan would occasionally take me to lunch. At the restaurant we'd sit and talk. Joan would give me feedback, such as working on certain ideas or trouble-shooting any problems. Instead of starting off the conversation with something like, "Hey Sandy, I didn't like the way you did this," she would start by pointing out my strengths. "Congratulations for always being on time. I know if there is a lobby call at 9:30, you'll be there by 9:25. I can always count on you to be prompt and ready to perform."

A gold record with Joan Jett, circa 1989

She'd also ask about my family. "How's your wife? Your daughter... how old is she now? Wow! That must be a fun age!"

Next, she would move on to my needs. "How's your drum tech working out? Is he doing all the things you need done? Your gear... how is it working? Is everything holding up with all the travel? Do you need anything from me?"

She'd ask about co-worker relationships on the road. "How are you getting along with the band and the crew? Anything happening I need to know about?"

She was concerned about me as a person. I was her drummer and her employee. She knew that my mental and emotional states were directly related to my work. She knew stressors in my off-stage life influenced my emotional states. Joan couldn't do anything about some of my difficulties, but she wanted to give me a chance to let her in on Sandy the Human Being as well as Sandy the Rock Drummer.

That quality of hers did not go unnoticed by me. Even if it didn't register consciously at the time, it left an imprint. It was inspiring, and it made me like Joan Jett even more than when I was a casual fan of her music, or when she hired me to be in her band. The more I liked and trusted her, the more I wanted to be in peak condition and perform my best for her every night, on every song, and on every note. She raised my level of enthusiasm and dedication to her success.

Joan Jett and I

Joan demonstrated another quality of an effective leader. She was professionally transparent, truthful, and honest with us without burdening us with business problems that had nothing to do with us. On a regular basis, she held team meetings with the band. Depending on the situation, we'd meet either as a large group or one-on-one.

Sometimes, she'd hold an impromptu meeting if we found ourselves walking together or sitting by each other on the bus. The impromptu meeting often consisted of a quick update on our progress. "Hey guys! We're close to platinum with the Up Your Alley album. We're doing really, really good!" Everyone shared in her enthusiasm, excitement, and pleasure with our work, and she would clearly state her mission: play hard, promote the album, and push it over 1,000,000 in sales.

CEOs and managers can learn a lesson from Joan: interest, dignity, and transparency are key. They are the ingredients to a successful business. When you run a small company, you have the unique opportunity to know all your employees individually. If you run a large company, you cannot have protracted sit-downs with each and every employee from the board room to the maintenance staff. Instead, you train managers and supervisors to engage and motivate their people with a positive mindset. Everyone in your organization is important. If they didn't play a vital role toward your company's success, their job wouldn't exist in the first place. Make sure your management team understands the importance of dignity and empathy when interacting with their respective employees.

I compare this to icing and cake. Everyone loves cake with icing—what's not to love? However, if the cake has too much icing, it tastes way too sweet and heavy. Conversely, if it's nothing but cake, it tastes dry and dull.

The same holds true for business. Think of the icing as the fiscal and less personal part of business. Spreadsheets, quotas, bar graphs, pie charts, analytics, money, raises, and benefits; the list goes on. The lifeblood of a business is profit. Without it, the business cannot survive. Important for sure, yet it cannot stand on its own.

Underneath all that icing is the structure that holds the icing up—the cake itself. The why behind the what. The cake is the personal and interpersonal part of the business, the relationships of the people behind the numbers. Cake is the foundation upon which we can serve up the icing.

Determining how motivation works with employees is an interesting science. Consider what keeps people engaged in a task. Typically, people put effort into a task they feel will lead to a reward. Take a slot machine, for example. If you've been to a casino, you've probably seen people who continually feed money into the machine. Even you, a rational person, might feel compelled to slide a few quarters more than you would expect into the one-arm bandit.

What makes the slot machine so powerful? The technical term is "variable ratio schedule of reinforcement." Put more simply, you get a little reward quite often and a big reward on rare occasion. But here's the catch: you never know when the payoff occurs. You might win a couple bucks on one play and feel the thrill of victory. Fueled by this extra oomph, you play a few more times because, even though you just won a little money, there could always be more waiting on the next pull of the handle! And the next, and the next, and so on....

Add to the anticipation of a payoff the commotion in the casino when some lucky soul on the other end of the room pulls a real jackpot. The crowd goes wild, and your head is filled with daydreams of how you would spend the $10,000 if you make the lucky pull!

Another handful of quarters later, you win a few, but lose a lot. You're busted, and you can't figure out why you stayed so long.

It's because you don't know when the reward would come.

What if you knew there was only forty dollars in the machine? Once you hit the forty-dollar mark, you would walk away: Mission accomplished. There would be no more incentive to keep going.

Allow me to return to McGregor's X and Y Theories of Management. If you recall, Theory X managers approach employees with the assumption that they are lazy, not too intelligent, and are only interested in a paycheck. A basic assumption of the Theory X model is that people are inherently self-centered, unmotivated, and avoid work whenever possible (McGregor, 1960).

If you're like me and think that enthusiasm and motivation are two sides of the same coin, you will easily see the problems with a Theory X approach. It quickly removes the joy and enthusiasm from the work environment, which invariably destroys motivation.

I call the people who manage this way "Bosses" instead of "Leaders." Bosses demand and dictate to strong-arm their employees into working. These Bosses mainly resort to negative modes of motivation, like punishment or fear.

This style puts an obvious emotional toll on employees. Ambient stress will wax and wane unpredictably throughout the week, or worse, remain at a constantly high level. This can manifest in interpersonal issues among employees (apathy, resentment, quarreling), or break down their immune reactions and lead to physical ailments, making them more vulnerable to illness.

What creates enthusiasm and motivation in your employees? If you agree it's money and fear, then you also agree your employees lose all motivation once those two goals are accomplished.

It's quite easy to imagine the effect of the fear-mongering Boss. Is she standing over the shoulders of her employees today? No? She's on vacation this week? Good! The cat is away, so there's no immediate fear in the mice. Therefore, little to no productive work gets done for a few days. As the Boss's return approaches, the pace of work might pick up a little because the fear is returning.

The same dynamic applies with the Boss who assumes an employee works out of a singular financial motive. If the job is relatively easy with no hard deadlines, employees under the Theory X Model will naturally slow down. No point in speeding up if the worker gets the same pay for less work.

Let's look at the converse: Theory Y managers. I call these folks "Leaders."

Theory Y posits that work can be internally reinforced and sustained if the conditions are favorable. If employees are committed to the organizational objectives and encouraged to relate to the company's goals as a basic part of their sense of fulfillment, then they will continue to put forth their best effort. The motivator (that internal satisfaction) isn't completely reached until the project is done and completed correctly.

How does a Leader achieve this condition and feed enthusiasm and engagement at work? By doing the following:

Be more transparent. Consult with employees regarding decisions that affect the business and/or the employee as an individual. Help them understand the mission of each project as it relates to the overall health of the company.

Help them feel valued and valuable. Delegate tasks; avoid micromanaging. Send the message that you trust the employees' capability to accomplish their tasks, including troubleshooting and resolving problems along the way.

Praise positive performances! Treat people with respect. Rather than emphasize only weaknesses or mistakes, lead with a core strength when evaluating an employee. Similarly, incorporate spontaneous moments of affirmation. Just hearing the Leader lean in and say, "You're really killing it today!" can provide a microburst of pride, and energize an employee to work harder for you. The same concept can apply to the whole employee group. Hold meetings every week or two to honor employees who have reached laudable achievements. Draw positive attention to employees in front of their peers to bring focus to the benefit of positive behavior.

Match employee's tasks to their skills with room for growth and expansion. This can keep the employees feeling competent and satisfy their need for challenge by broadening their horizons within the company.

As you look over these descriptions, realize that neither Theory X nor Theory Y Models work in isolation. For example, if you never paid your employees, they wouldn't stick around for long. Also, not everyone is completely motivated by self-actualization. The foundational belief of "if I don't do my work, I will lose this job," is already built into the employee mindset.

Instead, use a hybrid of these two theories. Compensate employees at fair market value and expect their best work but temper it by being a leader who is quick to compliment. Don't be the leader who makes employees feel like they are constantly in trouble. Feedback should be constructive and aimed at helping the employee better themselves and the company.

Create a collegial and interconnected atmosphere where people feel accepted and valued. Train employees well and trust their judgment. Help everyone understand that failure and human error are often unavoidable. But if it happens, take responsibility for your mistakes. Were the instructions not clear? Was the employee properly trained? Did you answer questions or regard their issues thoroughly? Doing so fosters respect for the Leader by the employees.

Everyone under your organizational umbrella is a critical piece of the company machinery. Each employee is a bundle of thoughts, feelings, energy, creativity, and ideas. Know the individuals and learn what makes each of them tick.

***

A huge difference between a Leader versus a Boss became evident during recent events. Many CEOs and business owners had to re-think how to conduct business when the COVID-19 pandemic struck.

When the virus hit, businesses were faced with a herculean challenge: how do we remain afloat during this time of commerce slowdown? Many small businesses didn't have the flexibility or cash on hand to keep the doors open. The owner may have been the only employee, or their immediate family worked the shop. A number of those businesses shuttered for good.

Medium to larger businesses also had hard decisions to make. They may have had the resources to remain solvent for the time-being. Despite that, they still had no idea when the world would return to a rate of commerce they were used to. They had to decide what needed to be done to cover expenses and keep their employees above water— if they could even keep employees at all.

When the pandemic hit, emotions were hit hard, too. It challenged the strength of all Leaders. A critical component of solid leadership is to remain objective and keep all emotional aspects in check. Allowing the thinking part of the brain to remain steady and the feeling part of the brain to remain quiet, allowing for better, clearer decision-making.

What did the Bosses do?

Of course, the Bosses panicked. Maybe the Boss sent out an email to all the employees, explaining that the business would only keep a skeleton crew. Names were listed, and the remaining employees were to arrive the following day with a box for their belongings. They were laid off with no hope of returning.

There's a lot to unpack here.

First, the method of communication was not personal. Email is a terrible way to break bad news to people. It suggests an air of disinterest, at best, and cowardice, at worst. Yes, people will be upset when you let them go. Not at the management, personally— after all, this is a global pandemic; it hit everyone on the planet. The employee may be upset because they are worried and terrified. They are wondering how to pay their bills without a steady paycheck. The Bosses did not have the common decency to take just a couple minutes per employee to empathize and be present during one of the worst times in recent history.

As you can see, the Boss takes a self-centered approach to managing a crisis. They go into retention mode and try to hold on to everything they can keep for themselves. In other words, "What's in it for me?"

Second, moving in the direction of the panicked Boss leads to anger and resentment from the employees who were laid off. Consequently, fear and lowered performance from the employees they retained became very evident. Employees made to come to the office and empty their desk will undoubtedly be commiserating with their friends who are also made to empty their desks. The Boss has fallen off everyone's Christmas card list.

Meanwhile, inside the building, the employees who still have jobs watch their former colleagues pack up their personal effects. They are curious, but also concerned: Who is next? Is the axe poised above me? Is the company going under? Do I need to find another job right this moment? Morale has taken a hit.

Fear and anxiety, whether intentional or not, inhibits performance. As the emotional part of the brain demands more thought space, it impacts the effectiveness of the rational thinking brain. Attempting to concentrate after receiving emotionally powerful news, good or bad, is nearly impossible. Judgment is swayed by emotions.

The converse of this managerial style would be innovation instead of hysteria. Leaders realize their team will eventually get everyone out of this. What did the Leaders do when faced with the pandemic?

When a Leader receives news that the company is failing and the world is shutting down for the time being, the Leader calls a company-wide meeting. They explain, in detail, the financial crisis happening to the company. They are transparent about the state of the business. During that meeting, the Leader remains in control of their emotions and stay in the present. They describe the situation in terms of reality but incorporate a positive slant.

They use phrases of encouragement, such as, "We can get through this," or "We will stick together as a team," inspiring a concerned workforce with hope—and hope is a powerful motivator! It leaves everyone with the impression that the Leader is in control of the situation. During any time of crisis, people seek the calming oversight of a competent Leader.

For many people, this mindset has its roots in childhood. When kids don't know how to read a situation or feel uneasy around a stranger, they look to their parent for reassurance. The parent—or in this case, the Leader—is the umbrella in the storm.

Of course, the financial side of the changes in business must be faced.

Once everyone is oriented to the Leader's sense of calm during the crisis, the Leader becomes solution oriented and initiates a more personal financial plan for each employee. The Leader arranges a one-on-one meeting with each employee. In larger corporations, the Leader meets with higher level management, who in turn, meet with their management teams, and so on down the line. The team connections will trickle down the ranks.

After all, you can say the sun is shining all you want, but if it's pouring outside, you're still going to get wet.

During the meeting, the Leader may say, "You were at the general meeting. You know about the financial situation we face. I don't want to lay anyone off. I am open to hearing your ideas and solutions. Is there anything you can do to help keep the doors open and help everyone stay employed? Would you be willing to forfeit a small part of your salary temporarily? Would you be willing to delay your vacation until next year, so I don't have to pay for a replacement or lose production while you're gone? Your input matters to me and the company."

Sometimes a Leader is required to make hard decisions on behalf of the company. Still, they must look out for the employees. Asking everyone to temporarily take a lower commission on their sales or give up overtime work and overtime pay can save the company money to keep everyone working. If this is asked of employees in a tactful and diplomatic way, no one feels as if they are being asked to give up more than anyone else. Everyone is in it together—and taking less pay for a year beats being out of work entirely.

I'm reminded of the closing scene in the movie It's a Wonderful Life. George Bailey (played by Jimmy Stewart) owns a bank named Bailey Brothers Building and Loan. It's on the brink of bankruptcy because of the dirty dealings of the evil Mr. Potter.

George has to solve a problem: there's going to be a run on his bank, and he does not have the cash on hand to cover the impending withdrawals of the townspeople. He contemplates suicide. Just in time, his guardian angel, Clarence appears to let him know how important his life is to those around him. With Clarence's help, George shakes off the emotions and formulates a solution.

George scrapes together all the cash he has and addresses the mob of frightened townspeople that have gathered in the lobby of his bank. He asks them for their help to keep the Building and Loan afloat. He is transparent about what has happened, and then he lays out his thoughts on what they can do to help. Everyone is challenged to figure out how much money they absolutely need to pay their bills. Rather than pull ALL their money out of Bailey Brothers, they only take out a small fraction of what they have in their accounts.

One by one, George and his employees distribute money to the people. Once their panic subsided—thanks to George's transparency and call to action—they balanced their financial needs at home to keep the Building and Loan alive in their town. When the emotion was put on the back burner, the decision was easy.

After the final withdrawal was made, George had two dollars left over. He locked the doors while his wife put the dollar bills in the vault. They remained in business. The townspeople recognized the crisis, learned what they could do to help avert the crisis, felt connected to George, and trusted his leadership. They were personally connected to the success or failure of the business; thus, they temporarily made a small sacrifice to achieve a big, shared goal.

Leaders lead. Bosses order. Leaders solve problems with a mindset geared toward dignity and respect. Bosses solve problems with a mindset geared toward themselves.

A Leader has the power to reward the sacrifice of their employees. Again, the plan is for the company to pull out of the crisis. The company has bought enough time to pivot and adapt to the changing consumer landscape of the post-COVID-19 society. The gift of the employees was the life-support the company needed. The Leader can show their gratitude in ways that are meaningful to the staff. For instance, if someone gave up their vacation days, the CEO could grant them extra days the following year. If they gave up a percentage of their commission, the CEO could grant them a few extra percentage points the following year. If they took a salary reduction, a nice bonus should be in order when the company's coffers fill back up.

This is a part of any relationship. You give for me; I give for you. If all the benefits in a marriage were experienced by only one partner, and all the sacrifices made only by the other, the relationship would destabilize in a New York second. The most stable and productive relationships are built with mutual respect.

If someone does you a favor, it makes you feel good. You'll want to return the favor. Yet, some people will ask for and never return favors. They may get what they want once or twice—but that will be the end of any good grace they will ever receive.

Your business is a long-term relationship. Treat it with respect.

***

To the readers who hold a management position, please keep this in mind: the more you micromanage your staff, the less likely they will be to engage in flexible thinking and adaptive problem solving. If you require employees to clear any and all new ideas or procedures with you before implementing, you slow down progress. They may decide that your hassle and your scrutiny isn't worth the effort of change. If you punish people for creative solutions that fail, they will no longer step outside of the box you leave for them.

Obviously, some limits must be placed on what employees can and cannot do. However, the more the reins are tightened, the narrower their path of creativity will be. When something goes sideways, the workforce won't be equipped to adapt because you have taught them to not adapt.

Encourage, reinforce, and reward creative problem solving and new ways of performing. If an employee tries something that doesn't work, show the employee that this is progress, and it's okay. Punishing or humiliating the employee in front of their peers only invites a major shutdown in solution-oriented thinking. Even learning what not to do can bring us toward solutions and create new ideas we never expected.

This holds true for the music industry, too. Let's say a guitar player's instrument gets damaged in transit to Spokane. Knowing guitar players like I do, they react as if a family member was just seriously injured. In the depths of their despair, the guitar tech, who is also the roadie, calls around and finds a place that rents guitars. The rental guitar that shows up might not be the exact model the artist wanted, but in the eleventh hour, it gets the job done. The artist might be thrown off a little by the change, but they'll be okay. However, now the whole team has a place to call when they need help with their gear in Spokane. They meet the shop owner and make a new connection in the eastern Washington music scene. Several new network opportunities could arise from the experience.

You never know.

If you, as a manager and a person, are uncomfortable with change, do your best to rein it in. You'll avoid stifling your team's adaptivity and creativity. And, if you're not careful, you yourself may learn to accept change.

Chapter 9: Relationships

To be an effective leader, you've got to develop a genuine, sincere relationship with your employees. Make them feel connected to the company and demonstrate for them an understanding that they are a part of the company's success. Build their energy and drive their enthusiasm.

When I look back over my career, I discovered that relationships are a non-negotiable aspect of my personality. If I am not kind to others, I don't feel as though my life is right. It doesn't matter if someone is an A-list celebrity or the guy who attends the men's restroom in the auditorium. I am equally kind to all of them.

Relationships are a huge part of who I am as a person, and they are almost single-handedly responsible for all my success. Yes, I'm pretty good at playing the drums. But so are a lot of other folks. Opportunities have come to me because of the relationships I've cultivated. Starting from Dave in the Doorway, life-changing dominos that fell for me were the result of so many strong alliances.

***

Craaft was a rock and roll band out of Germany. You may have never heard of them because they didn't make much of a dent in the American music scene. I encourage you to go to YouTube and check out their self-titled 1986 album. As rock albums of the mid-1980s go, it's not half bad. These musicians did good work.

The band consisted of three guys: a singer/guitar player, a keyboard player, and a second guitarist. They recorded their demo in Germany with a drum machine. One of the guitar players did double duty by playing bass on the recording. When Craaft was picked up by Epic Records, they had to hire a drummer and bass player to record the full album and go on tour.

That's where I came in.

Craaft's manager, Uwe Block, was partnered with an American management company to try to give them more international noticeability. Their music was solid, American-sounding rock and roll, so they figured it would be an easy transition. One of those American managers contacted me during the fall of 1985.

The manager met me in their office and asked if I would fly to Germany to help record the album. Honestly, the compensation package wasn't that great when compared to the work that needed to be done. I had to learn all the songs, travel to Europe, stay for over two weeks, and participate in the recording sessions. My gut instinct flew up a red flag; this could a gig I was not going to like.

Before officially saying no, I took a moment to really think about it. There were some upsides. Everyone I met who was connected to the project was cordial and gracious. They showed great enthusiasm for me, which made me feel appreciated. Also, I didn't have a lot going on at the time anyway, so I thought, Sure, why not? I said yes.

Off I went to Germany to record the album. I was paid less than scale for the project. Because I wasn't an official member of the band, I was paid as a contract worker. But they were so delighted to have me on board! It really raised my spirits because of their eagerness and welcoming attitude. Being comfortable with the band and knowing I was "their guy" were extremely important values to me. I like getting paid, sure, but appreciation is a commodity that rivals any financial compensation. When the album was finished, I returned home and returned to my regular life.

In January of 1986, Uwe Block called me again. "Hey Sandy! You did such an amazing job on the record. So amazing that we'd like to fly you back and do the tour with us."

This time, my gut instinct screamed. I turned him down. The album was one thing, but a lengthy tour of Europe for another small amount of money just didn't seem financially responsible. I needed, at least, a reasonable compensation to make it worth the time and energy it would pull from the rest of my schedule.

But that didn't faze Uwe at all. He called me a couple more times, and we went back and forth. Each time, he would up the offer and I would turn him down. I hadn't ruled out the possibility that he could come up with a number we could both live with, but I couldn't afford to compromise on what I felt was the base necessity to compensate me for my time, my skills, and my constitution on a tour.

On the third call, Uwe finally gave me the right offer. The other three members of the band agreed to cut me in at 1.5 points on the album. In other words, I would own "shares" of the album—I became a shareholder in the album's success. Each of the three members gave up ½ a point to woo me onto the tour. They really wanted me, and they put forth the effort to show it.

Their appreciation, their willingness to contribute, and their never-say-die attitude were big factors that influenced me to take the live gig. The band members sacrificed a part of their own earnings to show how important I was to their success. The dollars and cents didn't really matter, but their dedication truly did.

Craaft and I had our lawyers get involved to get the wording of the contract correct. The official offer sheet came to me, and I signed on to do the tour. To get ready for the event, I asked about the tour itself. Uwe replied with four words that nearly made me drop the phone.

"We're opening for Queen."

After I recovered my wits, I thought to myself, I would have done this tour for free!

It was 1986, one year after Live Aid. Freddie Mercury was in the process of coming out, and Queen was on top of the world. And the world was thrilled.

We did roughly five shows per week with Queen. The lineup for the large, open-air shows was generally Craaft, Marillion, Level 42, Gary Moore, and then Queen. Those shows were approximately

100,000+ fans at every venue. It took my breath away to be up there and face the pulsating sea of humanity on those nights.

We also had a series of shows at soccer stadiums, which were a minimum of 50,000+ fans every night. At many of those stadiums, we did two straight nights. The European Queen fans were not satisfied with a mere 50,000 tickets for one show. They routinely added a second night to squeeze in the fans that couldn't get a ticket for the first night.

That extra night gave me the chance to get out and explore the city. There wasn't a bus ride or even a sound check for the second night, so I didn't have to arrive at the venue until the early evening. Because I had that free day to walk the sights and take photographs of the historic cities in Europe, the Craaft tour became the most memorable tour of my career.

On the first night of the tour, I was hanging with Craaft in our dressing room after our set. There was a tap-tap-tap on the door. Standing in the doorway was Queen's guitar player, Brian May.

He said, "Hi, guys! Welcome to the tour. You sounded great out there. If you guys have any problems at all, I want you to come to me."

Goofing around with Brian May

He gestured toward his chest with his thumb, "Don't worry about the road manager or the production manager. You come to Brian, and I'll sort it out."

He also invited us to the after party. Queen was making EMI Records so much money back then, the label would close a disco or a club in every city they played and rent the entire venue for a private party. The location was always a secret; only band members and select members of management and crew were allowed to attend.

I hustled my butt to every one of those parties I was able to attend.

Roger Taylor and me then...

94

...and now

Queen was flying around on private jets; Craaft was on a bus. For that reason, we sometimes had to leave right after the show so we could drive overnight and arrive in the next city ahead of the show. When we were able to stay the night, I partied with Queen.

Brian was at almost every one of the parties, so he and I bonded after a while. Roger Taylor, the drummer, was at most of the parties as well. You never saw John Deacon, the bass player, at the parties—you only saw him when he walked from the dressing room to the stage and back. Freddie was at maybe 30-40% of the parties.

After being on the road for a couple weeks and hanging with Brain May at the after-parties, we became friends. At one of the parties, he leaned in and asked a question in his tight British accent, "Did you ever meet Freddie?"

I shook my head. No, I hadn't.

Brian gestured with his chin toward the bar area. There sat Freddie Mercury. Brian got up and motioned for me to follow. As we approached the bar, security made a path for us through the crowd like Moses parting the Red Sea. Brian introduced me to Freddie.

Freddie took my hand and gently shook it. With a graceful and soft-spoken voice, he said, "Very nice to meet you, Sandy. Your band sounds really good."

I was a bit taken off guard by his modest demeanor. On stage, Freddie Mercury was larger than life. He will always be one of the best examples of a consummate Rock Star in every sense of the word. His on-stage performance was unparalleled. But off stage, there next to me that night, he was a soft-spoken man with windows of vulnerability in his eyes.

He asked about my accent and where I was from. It was just chit-chat, but he took an interest in me and was very complimentary of the band. Just before I excused myself for the evening, I asked if I could take pictures of Queen while they were performing on stage. Freddie kindly agreed, asking only that, while I take the pictures, I remain out of sight.

Words cannot do justice to the tour de force that was Freddie Mercury. I set up my camera on the rear end of his piano, which was just out of view to the audience. I was able to get solid, clear close-ups of him as he sat at the keyboard and sang. The pictures came out perfectly, and I will always treasure them.

The Magic Tour was Queen's final tour with Freddie Mercury. He passed away in 1991, sending the rock and roll world into mourning. When the band reconvened to tour again in 1995, Paul Rogers took over the lead vocal duties.

***

I tear up a little when I think about this story. I sometimes feel like I should pinch myself to make sure I'm not dreaming. For the most part, I have enjoyed all the relationships I've formed along the way. Yet not all of my relationships have been perfect. Sometimes, a musician can damage the relationship with fans. One such breach of conduct I encountered is burned into my memory. Out of professional courtesy, no names will be mentioned.

I and my family were invited to attend a major concert at the Nassau Coliseum. The drummer of a top touring rock band invited us as his special guests and recommended we get together with him backstage after the show. The drummer was a friend of mine, and I've known him to be the nicest guy in the world.

The show that night was an unfortunate experience. The band did not perform as well as they normally did, and the crowd knew it. They didn't react in a way the band had liked. The reaction to the band was lukewarm, at best. As a result, the band didn't come out for an encore. Instead, they had their road crew come out and douse the crowd with big orange buckets filled with a certain super-sugary, fruity drink mix. Of course, my wife, daughter, and I were close enough to the stage to get hit with a full bucket of the stuff.

I and my family still went backstage after the show to meet my friend, despite being drenched. We waited around in the backstage area for over a half an hour. During that time, the fruit drink dried into a stiff and sticky mess on our clothes and our hair. My middle-school-aged daughter begged me to leave, but I was stuck. The drummer, a respected friend and music industry peer, had invited us backstage. It would be rude to blow him off.

He never showed. In fact, nobody in the band showed up backstage. And that felt rude to me. I don't believe for a minute his actions were personally against me and my family. However, if the band was butt-hurt, had a temper tantrum, and stormed out of the place, because of the audience's reaction, then they were childish. If the drummer forgot all about his backstage invitation and left us waiting for him, that's a big lack of professionalism on his part. I don't know exactly what happened, and I've never brought it up to him.

Whether I am in a huge touring band or my local cover band, I don't change how I treat people. If you are my guest, I go out of my way to ensure you are taken care of. If you ask for an autograph or a photo, I accommodate as well as I am able. I don't let success be my excuse; my internal moral compass is my guide.

Common human courtesy and respect are a universal concept often referred to as The Golden Rule. It is reciprocal—it goes both ways. You not only maintain consistent behavior regardless of your status, but you also don't treat people differently based upon their status. Fame and money do not matter—everyone deserves that basic respect.

I think of our soul as a little flame within us that makes us human. One goal of a relationship with anyone is to respect their flame; its heat is what will keep your own flame lit, too.

***

Ego is the enemy of success. I have made this my mantra for several decades. I try to make positive differences in people's lives, and I feel much of my success comes from the energy I give to others. When I speak to young musicians, I coach them to never use their abilities or fame (real or perceived) as an excuse to be a jerk.

I know the drummer I mentioned in the previous story didn't leave me in a lurch on purpose. But the outcome was still the same. We all have a network of family, friends, neighbors, and acquaintances in our lives. They toss us a life preserver when we feel like we're drowning. When they have trouble swimming, we need to throw them a life preserver, too, instead of an anvil.

Use your abilities to make someone happy. When you take the time and effort to help someone, you'll find that it makes you happy, too. Happiness moves in a circle—so keep it rolling!

Don't underestimate the perception another person may have of you. If you are a manager, leader, coach, church elder, or anyone else with a position of some power, you have a responsibility to treat people with dignity. When they aren't with you, they tell their family and friends about a cool interaction they had with you, this awesome person. Your thoughtfulness will spread.

Your words and actions affect those around you. I may be just the drummer in the band, but I would hate for someone to leave a venue and tell their friends, "Yeah...Joan Jett was awesome. But that drummer was such an asshole." This attitude doesn't just reflect on me, the drummer. It erodes the value of the brand that Joan Jett has worked so hard to build over her career. It's to her benefit to surround herself with good people who represent her well.

Leaders surround themselves with the same kind of people for the same reason. Put on the face you would like to see whether you walk into the boardroom, or you meet your daughter's dance instructor. Be aware of yourself and your presence.

I've never forgotten to be thankful for the opportunity to be famous. It's a gift. It took a lot of work on my part, but I never dismiss the effect of synchronicity and serendipity. Opportunity happens when luck meets preparation. A part of that preparation is your attitude toward yourself and those around you. Build relationships. Orient yourself to thinking within a positive mindset that guides you to treat others well.

***

When it comes to the stability of leadership through relationships at work, feedback and direction tend to be challenging moments. However, there's always a positive way to communicate any message. Even when assigning a task, the package in which you deliver the message is often more important than the message itself. If your words create pressure or defensiveness, the other person is less receptive to your message. If you approach with a warm and amicable attitude, they will receive your words in a relaxed and open manner, thereby raising the probability of success in completing the request.

For instance, imagine an employee standing next to a pallet of bricks as they wait for their assignment. A Boss will turn to the employee and say, "You've got until five o'clock to build a wall out of these bricks. I expect it to be done at quitting time, or else you'll be fired and replaced with someone who can get the job done. I've got a long line of people who want your job, so don't forget you're easily replaceable."

In other words, "Do it—*or else!*" What do you think that edict will do to the employee?

He's now under pressure. He may rush the job and cut corners to finish by five. He may feel resentment toward the Boss and do a sloppy job. He won't take pride in his work when he thinks his effort only makes the Boss look good—and he can't stand the Boss as it is! Why should he perform for a person who doesn't care about him and a job he feels no personal connection to?

Think about the message underlying the "do it or else" statement. The Boss indirectly communicated to the employee a negative expectation of outcome. If they operate under the belief that the employee will probably fail at the task (worst case scenario) or won't care one way or the other (best case scenario), then the employee will work to substantiate the Boss' opinion. A self-fulfilling prophecy is created. If the employee begins to believe he can't do the job (or do it satisfactorily), then his work will invariably drift in that direction.

Or the employee could rise above the interpersonal difficulties and complete the job in a timely manner. He may also complete the job to the best of his ability and build the best wall anyone has ever seen. That's an employee who is aiming much higher than this job with the Boss's pile of bricks. Unfortunately, this is a rare employee and a rare occurrence. Expecting a positive outcome by using negative methods is, in reality, an exercise in futility.

The best strategy, as always, is to be a Leader rather than a Boss.

The Leader would approach the worker standing next to the pallet of bricks and address him by name.

"Hey Jimmy! You're a really talented bricklayer. You do excellent work, and I know I can count on you to build a wall using this pile of bricks. I need the wall done by five o'clock, which I know should be no problem for you. Do your best! We're building a cathedral on this site, and I can't wait for people to look at the structure and marvel at your craftsmanship."

What do you think that approach does to the employee?

Now, he takes the time to do it right. Getting done by five o'clock may be a bit of a push, but he may work a few minutes into his lunch to make sure he gets it done. He probably won't go running to the time clock at 4:55 and stand around, waiting to punch out. He may work until 5:15 just to get it done right before he climbs into his truck and heads for home. The Leader has reminded him of what good work he does, which provides a boost in confidence and connection to his craft.

The Leader was attentive to the relationship between him, as the foreman, and the employee as a master bricklayer. The Leader also communicated the expectation of a positive outcome. In his mind, the bricklayer thought, my manager likes my work. He thinks I do a good job. For nearly any worker, that positive communication will inspire them to fulfill your expectation.

The Leader not only reminded, but showed enthusiasm for, the bricklayer and how others are going to view his work in the future. He, his family, and the whole community will look at the cathedral and feel proud of his craftsmanship. The sense of responsibility to himself and his community will make the employee feel personally responsible for the success of the project. His wall is only a part of, but connected to, a whole building that will be seen for generations. It allows them to understand the why behind the what.

Last, the Leader reframed the pressure of the clock. Yes, it's challenging to get the wall put together by five. But when the Leader reinforced how Jimmy is not only capable of finishing by five, but also that he can finish and build it well, he gave him his deadline in a positive way.

Clear communication (what must be done), managing the relationship (using his name and addressing him eye-to-eye), and transparency (this will be a cathedral—think of how important that is to the community) are all being used effectively and economically.

The Boss and the Leader each talked to the employee for thirty seconds, tops. It isn't a matter of taking extra time or burning extra effort. Both approaches require an equal amount of resources but will lead to potentially different outcomes. You get the best out of your employee when you nurture the relationship and create an atmosphere of the employee's importance and connection to the job.

As a side-guy musician, I've worked with (and heard a few horror stories of) artists who tell everyone in their camp that they're all replaceable, so they had better straighten up and fly right. If you make any waves, you're gone. Heck, I remember hearing an artist address the band with these exact words: "You guys are a dime a dozen." The musicians left the meeting thinking, "Oh…is that what he thinks of us?"

100

Sometimes a clear division is set between star and band. The star may travel in private jets and stay in five-star suites while touring. The band and crew may cram onto one small bus and sleep wherever they can find space to curl up and shut their eyes.

Okay. That's a bit of a stretch, but you get the point. The star who is a true Leader makes everyone on the team feel valued and respected. They do their best to bridge the gap between star and band. Some division may be unavoidable, but when it's overtly highlighted and exploited, the band ends up resentful and less likely perform their best. Further still, they may bail on the artist to take a lesser-prestigious, but more fulfilling gig with a more grateful artist.

***

Many of the suggestions I make come with the proviso that very few things change immediately. If you implement some of the solutions you learn from this book or one of my live events, I caution you to be prepared for some trial-and-error.

For example, your employees may not fully understand what it is you are asking of them. Even with the best of intentions, they may fail to meet your new standards or match your revamped criteria. Also, they may forget. People find themselves acting largely out of habit and routine when they are in a work setting, so new directions might run into the wall of routine.

As a matter of fact, it would surprise me if you didn't have to repeat your instructions a few times or remind your employees to do what is now asked of them. Use patience and empathy. They are not doing the wrong thing as a personal attack against you or your company. Nor are they automatically lazy or apathetic.

In all likelihood, they are doing their best and will adjust over time with some gentle nudging toward a new level of productivity and attitude. The way you approach their progress, whether it be fast or slow, will speak volumes to the strength of the relationship and to you as a leader.

I always think about marriage when I think about initiating change in a routine. When the concept of repetition and patience to complete the change process while minding the sanctity of the relationship comes up, I have a certain married friend I think of.

He and his wife had new carpeting installed in their house. His wife was proud of the carpet, and wanted to keep it nice, particularly because their youngest child was old enough to be outside most of the time. The little one had a habit of tracking dirt into the house. As a new rule of law, his wife asked that he and the child remove their shoes whenever they entered the house. The new rule made sense, and it made for a longer lifetime for their plush carpet.

The problem was that my friend had spent the first 45 years of his life walking around his house with his shoes on. It wasn't because of any particular reason; he just never thought to take them off.

From that point forward, it was maddening for his wife to remind him every time to take off his shoes in the house. He immediately complied when reminded, but the issue finally boiled over. His wife declared that she was obviously not important to him if he did not make it a point to remember the one simple request she made.

When he told me about the problem, I could see both points of view. Him leaving his shoes on wasn't meant to be an affront to her, nor did it mean that he was callous to the things she found important. I advised him to reframe the whole experience for his wife—take a different look at the situation using her point of view.

They engineered a solution by way of a reminder at the door. On the doorframe leading from the garage into the house, he put a little slash of red nail polish at eye level. Seeing the polish gave him a visual cue to take his shoes off. Thanks to a simple touch of red nail polish, a problem was solved, and a marriage was saved.

My friend's wife weathered through her brief period of frustration. She saw that, over time, his behavior changed, and they were both satisfied with the results. I'd bet a paycheck that he still occasionally forgets, but she writes it off to simple human nature.

Thinking of weather, relationships are a lot like trees. Under ideal circumstances, the tree grows toward the sky, thick and strong, filled with healthy green leaves. Sometimes, the tree may not have an ideal growth. The tree might start growing a little bit askew, with branches curling and winding to one side or another rather than straight up. Over time, this creates an unusually twisted tree.

To alter the misdirection, time and energy are required. You may pound a few stakes near the tree, fashion a harness rope inside a rubber hose around some of the branches to avoid damaging the bark and tie it off to the stakes. Stress is applied to the ropes. This action should encourage new growth in the proper direction.

Does the tree straighten up overnight?

Heck no! It takes time and continuous, gradual adjustments. As it begins to straighten up, you tighten the ropes again. Keep applying the stress so that force pulls the branch in the proper direction. The tree is watered and nurtured, but you pay attention to the changes, always guiding growth toward the goal.

In a similar situation, if you have a kid who needed braces growing up (or maybe you needed them yourself), you are very familiar with this concept. Those darn things stay on your poor kid's teeth for several years, with regular adjustments and tightening along the way. They hurt sometimes because the orthodontist makes sure there is always a little bit of pressure guiding the teeth toward the ultimate goals: a straight smile in your kid's mouth, and a new swimming pool in your dentist's back yard.

Occasionally, this example makes me wonder if I went into the wrong profession.

As a Leader, you should empathize with your staff's mistakes, especially when they're distracted, overwhelmed, or fatigued. Rather than punish, a Leader becomes part of the solution, an agent of change. Teach, engineer, and mentor employees toward the shared goal of running the business smoothly.

***

To all the CEOs reading this book: It's not always about the spreadsheet or the bottom line. It's about relationships and leaving the world a better place than you found it. It's how your business gets both the icing and the cake.

The search for the best personnel who have the strongest company connection can be a rewarding endeavor with the proper positive mindset.

The culture of your company is an aspect of relationships that is critical to success. The employee who fits in as a team member is invaluable. Personality is an asset that is influenced by both biology and environment. It takes more than a big college degree or many years of experience in a chosen field. If you find a candidate who's well-suited for your company, it's worth paying them the right compensation. Your goal is to get that person to sign on. It sure beats the alternative of trying to jam one ill-fitting person after another into the role. Both time and money are wasted in such a short-sighted endeavor. My grandmother used to call it, "…being penny-wise, but pound foolish."

A good starting question for the interview is, "Why do you want to work for my company?" Take a moment to discern whether or not they are only searching for a paycheck. If they are, you know they may bail on you the second the shop down the street offers them an extra 80 cents an hour. Then the hiring and training process begins all over again.

However, if they give an answer that's not littered with only dollar signs, you have the makings of a loyal employee. Do they give answers that align with your company's mission and values? Did the answer show that the interviewee researched your company? Does the person seem genuine and authentic? If you find the answer is "yes," congratulations! You may have found an employee who will be with your team for the long run. You have made a good choice because this person likes your company and will be grateful for the opportunity.

Grandma would have called that a win-win.

***

I'm certain a few of you reading this book may think, "Yeah, that's all well and good. But what about that one problem employee who just doesn't seem to get it?"

Great question! Much of my presentation is about motivating employees to feel connected to the cause, then using the positive momentum from relationships at work to do their best. I look at the "big picture" philosophy. Please believe this: the big picture philosophy will work. Human nature shows that we try to please the people to whom we feel most connected to, and we most like.

If an employee seems to be falling off the pace, the big picture ideology can still be used to solve an individual problem. Let's say we have an employee who isn't meeting sales goals. Like many of your sales team, he has a quota he must match each quarter, and he has struggled to boost his declining numbers.

At this point, the manager has a couple choices. He could play hardball: "Get your numbers over the line or else I'll have to replace you."

Or he can try my approach.

As shown in many earlier examples in this book, the hardball approach might work in the short run. Some people can be motivated to stop the discomfort of pressure, or the looming "axe" hanging over their tenure with your company. From a long-term standpoint, you will probably lose that employee. He may not feel valued or may grow to dislike that manager as a person. Whatever the reason, he's out of there as soon as he can find a new gig.

It is quite possible that his current role in the company is a mismatch for his particular skill set. It is also possible that he began this job with great anticipation, only to find performing the job didn't meet those expectations. Maybe his life circumstances have changed, and he just doesn't feel the passion for the job the way he once did.

There is no shame in leaving a bad situation. But well before reaching that conclusion, some questions need to be asked. Let's incorporate the philosophy of personal relationship, transparency, and positive reinforcement to the scenario.

The CEO or direct manager should take the employee out to lunch. He will probably be nervous, given the general nature of the "we need to talk" vibe. But, if your company truly stays consistent with the positive reinforcement model, he should be confident that, despite his trepidation, this meeting will turn out fine.

At lunch, stay away from negative conversation for the first few minutes. Allow him a chance to relax and settle into a good conversational rhythm. Find out what makes him tick. He may bring up the topic of the sales figures first to get ahead of the conversation and relieve his own inner tension as he waits for the other shoe to drop.

Remember how I said Joan Jett would chat with me during lunch? It felt like small talk, but it was an important part of maintaining open lines of communication and relationship stability.

Try asking him about him. Ask how he is doing. You can float simple, inoffensive questions like, "So, how are things with you?" Let him take the lead on the direction he wishes to take from there. Current HR policy should require that all employees maintain a professional distance, no matter what role they have within the company. If he takes the initiative to bring up his kids, spouse, parents, or any other aspect of his personal life, tactfully engage. Don't be intrusive and make it seem you're prying—rather, be genuinely interested.

We all understand the value of the work-life balance, but few could argue that one does not have a profound effect on the other. Heck, if hating your job brings stress back home and affects relationships with family, it certainly stands to reason that stress at home can have an impact on focus, concentration, energy, or motivation at work.

If he seems troubled in any way, ask if there is anything the company can do within reason to help. That simple gesture may unlock some motivation—the employee now feels important and valued.

If all checks out okay, then ask about the job. I would caution you against being the one to bring up his low numbers; he knows. More importantly, he knows that you know. No sense poisoning the well and putting him on the defensive.

Your position when asking about the job should be one of curiosity and interest. Is there something he needs to help him perform at the level to which he knows the company expects? Conversely, is there anything standing in the way of his success?

My guess is that he would not have been hired into your company unless you or your hiring manager predicted he would be a welcome addition to your team. If his numbers have gone from good to subpar, what changed? More importantly, did anything change that you can help bring back in line?

If there doesn't appear to be anything of value you can provide to him, finish the lunch on a positive note. Take a few minutes and think about something that can act as a catalyst for positivity and motivation. Remind him that he has the tools to make this work, and you only want the best for him. As always, reinforce the good.

This idea came to me from a CEO following one of my live seminars. Obviously, the details have been altered to mask any identifying characteristics of the story, and your mileage may vary. But take it for what it's worth.

The CEO said that he had a team member who wasn't meeting his sales quota. The direct manager in the situation discussed options with the CEO. He could have given the employee a verbal or written warning. If the company and the employee both operated in a "right-to-hire" state, they could simply "lay him off," let him collect unemployment, and the company hires a new salesperson to take his place. He could suggest the salesman attend sales boot camp. Nobody liked sales boot camp for many valid reasons. The main one being that it wasn't a tool to help the salesperson—it was just a form of punishment.

The CEO thought about these options. He knew that if warnings or other punishments were used, the employee would work to get his numbers up solely to avoid the consequences. He wouldn't have cared about the company or anything ancillary to that minimum sales figure, such as taking care of the customer following the sale, following up on leads, or creating a positive work environment. Stressed out employees narrow their focus on survival, thus prohibiting behavior relevant to a broader caretaking of the company and/or the other employees. In a word, it is a short-sighted approach to prioritizing performance over morale.

Instead, the CEO suggested using compassion and empathy to help the salesperson with his motivation. He urged the manager find out why the salesperson was having so much trouble with generating sales, then look at solutions that directly solved the problem. The CEO suggested the manager do some info-gathering by finding space in his schedule to have a non-stressful, one-on-one discussion with the salesperson.

The manager took the suggestion and invited the employee to lunch.

During light conversation, the manager learned a bit about his salesman's life outside of the office. They talked about sports teams they both liked, and a little about the salesman's family. At one point, the salesman disclosed that his teenage daughter was a huge Taylor Swift fan. They laughed as the salesman recounted walking into his daughter's room and seeing her hanging the fifth or sixth Taylor Swift poster on a wall.

The issues with the employee's sales numbers didn't enter the lunchtime conversation. The manager ended lunch on a high note. There was no stress, no chatter about anyone getting fired or sent to sales boot camp. Instead, the manager returned to the office with a valuable piece of information that might lead to a win-win for the company and for the salesman. Already some goodwill was built from the personal lunch outing, but the manager had an even bigger idea up his sleeve. He made some phone calls.

About a week later, at the employee's home, a small package arrived. Tucked in a nondescript envelope were two tickets and VIP passes to an exclusive meet-and-greet with Taylor Swift. The salesman was confused, but in a good way. It took him a moment to fully digest what he was holding in his hands.

He shook the envelope, and out fell a short note, hand-written by the manager.

Hey Robert —

Take your daughter to the Taylor Swift concert.

Have a great time!

In an instant, the salesman was over the moon! Not that he was particularly interested in the musical stylings of Taylor Swift, but he had just become his daughter's hero. He took his daughter to the concert. She met Taylor after the show, got her autograph, and posed for a quick selfie with her idol.

Bear in mind, this situation relied on Taylor Swift coming to town reasonably soon after the lunch meeting between the salesman and his manager. But the conversation wasn't completely random or coincidental. The reason his daughter's love of Taylor came up in the first place was because the concert was looming close. The tickets and passes provided by the manager far exceeded the experience provided by any tickets her father would have been able to purchase on his own.

In short, this was a home run.

What did this act of compassion do to the employee's motivation to hit his sales figures? There was no discussion about having the tickets contingent upon sales figures or what the salesman would have to do to earn them. These were a gift because the manager knew he could do something positive for the employee and his daughter.

Obviously, there are no guarantees in life. The manager, acting on the advice from his CEO, took a chance and did something altruistic for the salesman. There was nothing asked in return, and no looming expectation of repayment or enhanced work performance.

The salesman's numbers ended up going through the roof. The CEO who told me this story was excited to share how his story lined up so perfectly with the message I was sending. The renewed enthusiasm those tickets generated in the salesman translated directly to his performance, as he wanted to do right by the manager.

In all, the tickets and the accompanying VIP passes cost the company about six hundred bucks. However, the resulting spike in the salesman's numbers—both short and long term—put thousands and thousands of dollars to the company. That was one heck of an ROI (return on investment)! The salesman felt valued, connected, appreciated, and appreciative.

Remember those words.

Value. Connection. Appreciate. Appreciative.

If you can cultivate a work atmosphere that is heavy in those four qualities, then you will have a staff who's long-term, happy, and motivated.

***

Corporate executives—challenge yourselves! Do you know the name of the newest intern in your office? The name of the security officer at the front desk of the office building? The name of your best customer's or vendor's administrative assistant?

Try this simple exercise for a week: The next time you go grocery shopping, catch the name of the person working at the checkout. Most store employees wear name tags, so this shouldn't be too difficult a task. Then ask them how their day is going. Pay attention to how they react—it's an interesting study in human interactions.

For some, the cashier behind the register or the deli personnel slicing your lunchmeat will give you a thoughtful response. In my experience, the more genuinely I ask, the more genuine the reply.

For many, however, they'll give you a common, superficial answer.

"Good."

"Okay."

"Fine. How are you?"

Some poor souls might even be on autopilot and say something out of place, like "Thank you."

Whatever their reply, don't accept the mindless response. Do a second lap with them to show you're not looking to check the "friendly conversation" box. Show that you are genuinely interested. Break through the robotic response and ask a follow-up.

"Doing good, huh? What was the good thing that happened to you today?"

You may need to practice your tone ahead of time. Make sure you don't come across as creepy or condescending, nor should you sound demanding or confrontational ("Tell me what happened..."). But if you are genuine and earnest in your approach, you will probably be met with a blush or a smile. People aren't accustomed to such a warm, personal touch these days. We slide past each other with superficial greetings and semi-rhetorical questions.

It's understandable. If we're out and about in the world, we assume nobody has the time to really engage each other. But look at it this way: Opportunity hides within that excuse. To ask a genuine question doesn't take all that long. If the teenager bagging your groceries answers you honestly, they may something like, "I got an A on my English test this morning."

109

You don't have to hover and take up much of his workday. You can say something affirming like, "Hey! That's cool! I was never that good in English class when I was your age. Way to go!" Then let it be done at that.

What you created was a genuine conversation that required you both to pay attention. You probably lifted each other's spirit, even if only for a moment.

This entire exchange you just read takes less than fifteen seconds to execute. Go ahead and time it; you'll see. It doesn't have to be a waste of valuable time—you can have the brief conversation during the time you would be waiting for the teen to put your bags in your cart, anyway. Why not pass the time connecting with a fellow human being instead of checking your phone for the latest Facebook post from someone you went to high school with several decades ago?

To expound on this concept, corporate executives can practice this skill with their managers and employees. Brief interactions with your staff can help build relationships, goodwill, and desire to work toward the mission of the company.

Conversation is like a muscle. You can practice and make it stronger with time and repetitions. Don't let your people skills atrophy or become disposable.

Some people call it "the gift of gab," but the ability to be genuinely interested in people has paid off time and time again in my own life. Chatting for an extra minute with the front desk clerk at a hotel creates a feeling of reciprocal goodwill. I have received a few room upgrades or little tokens of appreciation, like an extra snack from the goodie basket, just because I was nice to the clerk. It's the same with employees at any level of the service industry: wait staff, hostesses, the person behind the rental car counter, and so on.

I never make it a goal to try to extract deep information from the folks I chat with. Instead, I'm always up for a little light conversation while the other person and I are both sharing this space, for this heartbeat, in the grand scope of time.

Challenge yourself to approach and engage people at this level. Do it as a basic approach to treating others well, not as a strategy to get ahead or get one over on the person. It should be unconditional—if you expect something in return, the other person (and the universe) will feel that motive and react to it.

Just as good begets good, friendly begets friendly.

Chapter 10: Tenacity

When you've got belief in your goal and the people around you, you've got the tenacity to overcome the obstacles standing between you and the goal. Many times, the difference between success and failure is persistence. Stick-to-itiveness is fueled by tenacity; a belief that you will not give up until the goal is achieved. A synonym for tenacity in the business world is motivation. How driven are you to see a project or a goal through to the end?

Tenacity is a quality inherent to every great leader. It not only motivates them and the people around them, but it also allows them to overcome adversity. Tenacious leaders hold fast, determined to help the team achieve their goals and give purpose to their strength.

Often in life we feel as if achieving a certain goal is just too difficult. Accomplishing that goal is going to require effort and hardship—prepare yourself in advance for this reality. If you've ever set a goal to complete a home-improvement project, you've been forced to make your peace with the fact that you'll be making a minimum of three trips to the local hardware store before all is said and done.

The old cliché of finding a needle in a haystack speaks to this futility. But trust me: the needle is in there. Once your sleeves are rolled up and you are ready for the task at hand, you proceed with tenacity. You don't necessarily need the cunning of Odysseus, the strength of Hercules, or the riches of Midas to find that needle. Rather, you need the persistence of the Little Engine That Could. You keep going through that haystack, piece by piece, and you will get that needle.

When others give up, you are still there, on your hands and knees, sifting through the hay and straw until you find the needle. You can do it alone or surround yourself with people who share your mission. Motivate your employees and coworkers to engage in your vision—encourage them to want that needle. They may not want it as much as you do, but if they feel like a part of the project, they will grunt alongside you. They'll cherish the victory when the needle is held high, and fireworks explode in the distance.

Frustration is the enemy of success. I don't know where I was when I first heard that saying. I do know it hit me hard and remains in my mind when I feel my motivation start to wane. Also, when I start to waver, I think about the words of Thomas Edison, when asked about how many tries it took to finally invent the light bulb: "I never failed. I simply found 10,000 ways that won't work."

***

Sometimes, a leader's tenacity will intimidate or push away the people battling alongside them. Good sports coaches squeeze every second out of the clock or out of every pitch thrown, but if the team thinks of the coach as fanatical, incompetent, or maniacal in their pursuit of victory, the coach will "lose the team." They will no longer perform for the coach.

Coaches, therefore, are faced with the same task as every CEO or manager: how to motivate their employees to operate at their peak performance without alienating or "losing" them. Note that "losing" the team is not the same as irritating or annoying them. Frustration and discouragement are a part of both the learning curve and the success plan for every CEO. Managing employee frustration goes back to an earlier theme of mine: Nurture the relationships you form. Listen actively and react to the changing needs of the people in your company.

I understand that every leader feels that the people they manage can always give a little more effort. However, you can just as easily give five minutes of relief to your employees in order to gain hours of motivation and tenacity from them. Connect when your employees communicate that they're tired, angry, or discouraged. Validate them: "I get it, everyone. This is rough today. Let's take a five-minute break to shake off that last (fill in the problem), and come back ready to brainstorm some solutions!"

Strive to overcome the obstacle, but more importantly, take care of the relationship with your employees first. Let them know you are focused on their experience as well as the task. You "lose the team" when your tenacity eclipses the people helping you toward victory.

Psychologists have a term called learning through adversity. Every obstacle provides an opportunity to grow. That may sound like an empty platitude, but it's a very real experience. It can be a challenge to reprogram your mind to think tenaciously, but it is critical to model this mindset for your staff. Leaders will also coach the staff to achieve a similar mindset. Teach employees that clearing a hurdle gives them a better understanding of the problem and solutions. If nothing else, they have all learned what doesn't work, just like Thomas Edison. Clearing that hurdle will also increase their self-efficacy because now they have participated in success. More self-efficacy raises self-esteem, which in turn provides a stronger impetus to overcome future obstacles.

Again, a home improvement project makes a good analogy. You want to replace the faucet on the kitchen sink. You've got the new faucet, you've gathered the necessary tools, and you have watched the requisite YouTube videos. If you think you'll have the new one in place and cinched down in an hour, you're probably in for a major disappointment. Invariably, the wrench won't quite fit, you'll be missing a small piece of PVC pipe, or the faucet will be a little too big or too small to nest in the existing sink's cut-outs.

You make phone calls to your relatives who have done this before. Without fail, you will make additional trips to the hardware store, and then fiddle with it some more, maybe expanding the existing holes with a small grinder. Throughout the weekend, you do whatever it takes until the blasted thing fits.

The job you thought would be done by noon is finally done at six p.m. the following day, but you have (a) learned a heck of a lot about replacing a faucet, (b) made a new friend at the hardware store, and (c) felt an even greater sense of accomplishment because you overcame several obstacles, thus making the sweet fruit of victory even sweeter.

Maybe your spouse or child is helping you with the faucet. Are they going to be next to you in the foxhole if you snap at them or belittle them? Will they continue to be your ally if you treat them like a lightning rod to absorb your frustration? Obviously not.

A sense of humor, positive strokes, and having them think through the problem-to-solution paradigm with you will keep them motivated to remain by your side. Plus, they will feel just as good as you when you flip the lever at six o'clock Sunday evening and water comes out. And for all the parents out there, you have also taught your child to stick with a project instead of giving up at the first sign of trouble.

I think of catastrophic fails as a sign from God. By "catastrophic," I mean a failure that signals the genuine end of the road for a project. If you're not religious in this way, think of it as Karma, a sign from the universe, or c'est la vie.

I've encountered a catastrophic failure in my career, and it had an enormous impact on my life. I don't mean that in a trite, overly dramatic way—it truly changed the course of my life. However, it also helped me notice my own inner strength. I learned, beyond the shadow of a doubt, that I carried the tenacity to succeed in this tough, competitive industry.

***

113

In a previous chapter in this book, I mentioned a guy that Carmine Appice introduced me to: Earl Slick. He is an accomplished and skilled guitarist who has collaborated with David Bowie, John Waite, John Lennon, and many others. Early in my development as a professional drummer, Earl was one of my first critically important professional relationships.

Soon after I moved from New York to Los Angeles, Earl invited me to a big Hollywood party. He wanted to help me network with other musicians and maybe generate some leads to audition for bands around the area. At the party, I befriended a guy named Gary Grainger. And at that time, Gary was Rod Stewart's guitar player.

A few months after the party, Gary called to tell me that Rod Stewart was auditioning drummers to tour behind his A Night on the Town album. That was the album that included the #1 single, "Tonight's the Night," so this was going to be a monster tour.

It was also the song used for the audition. The audition itself was held at Studio Instrument Rentals (or SIR) on Sunset Boulevard. SIR made its mark on the music industry by leasing out backline equipment: amps, speakers, and drums. They also rented professional rehearsal studios. At that time, SIR was a standard in the music industry.

I was so excited that I made a grave mistake.

It was a cattle-call audition. When I walked in, there were three or four other drummers in the lobby waiting to be called. I could hear a drummer already in the studio begin to play "Tonight's the Night."

If you're not familiar with the song, it's got a nice swingy, shuffling sound. All the equipment required for the drummer's part in the song is a high hat, a snare drum, and a bass drum. Nothing complicated; the perfect song to assess a drummer's sense of rhythm and ability to keep time.

When my name was called, I got up and headed for the exit to the parking lot. The person coordinating the audition ran to stop me. "Oh! No, Sandy! The studio is this way!"

I turned to him. "I know. But I want to go get my drums."

"No," he chuckled. "You don't have to get your drums. We have drums set up in the studio already."

Out of insecurity, I wanted to set up and play my own drums. This was an important audition; the most important one of my young career. I certainly didn't want to leave anything to chance by playing someone else's drum kit.

Because I was stubbornly focused on me, I ignored what the coordinator was hinting at.

To this day, I swear, I want to kick myself in the butt to the point of pain for what I did.

I made Rod Stewart wait for me.

I trotted across the parking lot and unloaded the massive trunk of my 1963 Lincoln Continental. I lugged my double-bass drum set into the studio and set it up while everyone stood, staring in amazement.

Rod Stewart didn't stay long. He saw me hauling the rig in and uttered only one sentence to me. "Those drums better sound good, mate."

With that, he walked out.

I knew in an instant that I had screwed everything up before playing a note.

I was a determined trooper, though. I set up and played "Tonight's the Night." Then I disassembled my gear and left, my head hanging low.

Like many people, I'm my own worst critic. But this one was well-deserved.

I went home as depressed as I have ever been in my life. I was already growing disenchanted with Los Angeles, but this was the rotten cherry atop an awful sundae. I was at the lowest point I can remember, and I was about two seconds away from throwing my drumsticks into the fireplace.

***

In my mind, that was a catastrophic failure. That was the end of me ever playing for Rod Stewart, and I knew it. I'm not going to lie—it sucked. I was alone, demoralized, and had three figures in my bank account, which includes the two after the decimal point.

In hindsight, I reconfigured how I viewed that moment.

Maybe God knew it wasn't quite the right time for me to get the gig. Maybe I wouldn't have done well on the road with Rod. Maybe I needed to feel the frustration so I could learn that I had it in me to persevere. Or maybe—and this is how it turned out—I had to not get the Rod Stewart gig so I would double down on my efforts to throw a Hail Mary pass, and land better gigs in New York.

I had to learn tenacity.

It helps to remember that failure is short term. You can view it as a part of a bigger plan, even if the plan isn't apparent at the time.

Leadership requires the mindset of "never say die" while still maintaining relationships. Leaders motivate, which is always better accomplished with positive attitudes and beliefs than shame and punishment.

I overcame the Rod Stewart setback. Every successful person has had to overcome adversity. It's part of the plan.

***

Cyndi Lauper, as an artist and as an entertainer, is the very embodiment of tenacity. She simply would not take no for an answer. She was headstrong, for sure, but she was also a problem-solver who made sure to exhaust all options before giving up on a vision. When everyone else would walk away from an idea because it seemed outlandish or impossible, Cyndi would dig in and give it one more round. She was determined—a clear ingredient of her success.

Her overall attitude was always one of positivity. If she could imagine it, she wanted to do it. More than that, she never thought she wouldn't be able to do it. For her, it was a matter of how, not if.

Her intersection between creative vision and determination happened October 10, 1984, at the Houston Summit (later renamed the Compaq Center, now the Lakewood Church Central Campus, home to Joel Osteen's mega-church). The Bangles opened for us during that leg of the tour, and we were set to record a live music video behind the single, "Money Changes Everything."

Under normal circumstances, the entire concert would be live. But, as it was for many bands of that era, the song for the video would be a background track. The band and the artist would lip-sync the track while the cameras rolled and captured the video footage. Later, in the editing and production process, the audio track would get superimposed back over the performance, and we would have a nice, clean music video.

That was normally how things were done. However, this was Cyndi Lauper.

She decided that she wanted the band to play the music. She didn't want a background track of the album version, so the audio capture would be our actual live performance. That was all well and good, but it put a lot of pressure on the band to be perfect in the performance.

Specifically, that put a lot of pressure on me. When a drummer is "on," he or she can play as flawlessly as a metronome. But in a live performance, anything can happen. Musicians will tell you of the little quirks, errors, and detractions from precision. It happens. But it couldn't happen on this night.

Then, Cyndi upped the ante.

She went to David Wolff and told him she wanted to do something crazy but pre-planned —something that had never been done before. She wanted to go up and fly over the audience, suspended by cable… in a garbage can.

David thought she had lost her mind.

She was positive it could be done. They just needed to come up with a solution. They needed to invent a how. Her motto: "If the mind can think it, we can do it. Conceive, Believe, Achieve."

She was told it absolutely could not happen. But she wouldn't let it go. She blew right past, "It can't be done," and entered, "Let's figure out how."

I love that about her.

Lo and behold, they found a way. NFL Films came in to shoot the video, and their engineers and riggers figured out a suspension system that allowed Cyndi to (a) fly above the audience in a garbage can while singing, and (b) capture the whole performance on film.

It was the first music video ever filmed by the NFL Films crew. It was also the first time they used the remote cable cameras in a venue other than a football field. The whole thing worked.

Go check out the video on YouTube. Search for "Cyndi Lauper - Money Changes Everything (Live)," and at 4:40, you can see Cyndi hop into her garbage can and get lifted over the crowd. It's not something you'll see every day of your life.

***

One adage in the world of business is, "If you want to get something done, give it to a busy person." I don't know who said it, but they sure knew how powerfully true it is. You may know a few people yourself who "get things done." Likewise, you may know others whom you avoid when something needs to be done. They'll put it off unless you continue to "dog and nag" them about it. Another power in this saying is that it's counter intuitive. It makes no sense that people who are constantly moving and taking on projects will get to your request faster than someone with very little to do.

What the heck is that about?

Perhaps we can take a basic principle from Newtonian physics: The Law of Inertia. A body in motion tends to stay in motion. A body at rest tends to stay at rest. The physics idiom implies that any physical object remains unchanged unless it is acted upon by a separate force. If a tennis ball is thrown toward the garage door, it stops the tennis ball's forward flight.

So, what then, is this force that slows some people down and speeds some people up?

Motivation. Tenacity.

During the hiring process, managers are constantly trying to assess the level of motivation in their prospective employees. The more accurate your appraisal, the more valid your decision will be when you extend an offer for employment. Unfortunately, research has shown this to be a difficult personality variable to accurately assess in the short form of most job interviews.

Rather than go over assessment tools for motivation or personality, which most HR departments should already have, let's look at how to improve the motivation of employees once they are already hired and functioning within your company structure.

Having an internally motivated employee is the prize every manager seeks. Once you have a person like this in place, the trick is not to wind them up and let them go. The trick is to keep them wound up and going in the right direction. That means arranging the teams such that you don't allow poorly motivated employees to chip away the resolve of the highly internally motivated worker.

Arrange teams so that each one has its own highly motivated member. More than one per team can work if their methods don't compete, but that is a difficult balance to maintain. However, one highly motivated individual can take the lead on a project and rally the troops to balance the remaining team members.

Populate the remaining team spots with as many moderately motivated members as you can. Their energy will vary, but the highly motivated team lead can coordinate everyone. They recognize their own contributions but maintain the option of backing off while another moderately motivated teammate takes over. Volleying the bigger tasks to these employees will ensure the task gets completed without burning out or creating resentment among the team.

Finally, reserve one spot for a poorly motivated team member. I know companies try their best to weed out employees who seem to have trouble pulling it together. Reality dictates that your management team will invariably use their energy to support those team members.

If you assign two or more low motivation employees onto one team, they may begin to reinforce each other's behaviors. Ultimately, they could undermine the efforts of the leader by slowing down rather than speeding up. The more toxic version of this scenario would be that they frustrate the highly motivated employee, creating burnout and/or a desire to abandon the team and the project altogether.

However, a single low-motivation person on a team can learn from the example demonstrated by the rest of the team. Should they ally with a moderately motivated teammate who will reshape their passivity, the overall dynamic of the team can put them back on task. The environment will be one of collegiality and forward progress rather than stagnation and disruption.

If the team is structured properly, the reinforcement feedback loop will keep everyone oriented toward the goal. This can change the way the low motivation person thinks or feels. After all, if productive behavior is reinforced and stalling behavior is not, then their best option will be to march in stride with the others.

Keep in mind that, for the most part, most humans are uncomfortable with being a discrepancy. Deep inside, we all seek to belong and be accepted. A natural tendency for most will be to work within a group rather than knowingly act like a disruptive jerk who wants to be ostracized.

***

The most satisfying reward for a task well done is the recognition of the achievement. Lauding an employee both privately and publicly gives them an internal satisfaction and pride. The self-esteem you've boosted will drive their motivation.

Perhaps you've heard the saying, "praise in public and criticize in private." Learn the power of a swift, but personal, "way to go" when you pass the employee in the hallway. Lean in and give them a quick word of affirmation at their workstation. Those thoughtful moments of congratulations can bolster motivation.

119

Some employees may find being praised in public awkward and a bit anxiety-inducing. Concerns arise if it leads to negative backlash from their peers. Resentment and envy are very real issues in companies, both large and small. Management should make sure to publicly praise for quantifiable achievements. Do so on a predictable and consistent basis and spread it out among the group. Everyone should feel like the entire organization is made up of people pulling on the same rope. It will cultivate an atmosphere of positivity rather than negativity.

Frame praise and achievement in terms of an employee's effort and productivity rather than luck. Nothing makes me crazier than hearing a high-achieving person ramble on about how lucky or how blessed they are! I am absolutely not discounting that luck happens in any career. The music industry is filled with a sea of outstanding musicians who work hard their whole life—yet, neither you nor anyone else will ever hear their name. Numerous musicians who aren't necessarily proficient at their craft will fall into a good situation and became household names. Life is a crap shoot sometimes.

My frustration happens when the assumption is made that the only reason the celebrity is notable is because of luck. The message underneath those words is, "Don't bother working hard, being tenacious, or perfecting your craft. If you just get lucky, then you'll be rich and famous!" This is what American Idol has put into many people's minds. All you need is unwitting luck, and you'll achieve all your goals.

I remember cringing when I learned that one of my beloved New York Yankees, a pitcher named Lefty Gomez, once proclaimed, "I'd rather be lucky than good."

What?!

With all due respect, Mr. Gomez, luck only takes you so far! Lefty himself was a major league ball player for thirteen years—hardly a stroke of luck. When Lefty Gomez first entered the major leagues, his pitch speed had great velocity. He was thin scrapper of a man, only six foot two and 155 pounds. He had one hell of a powerful arm, but he lacked the stamina to maintain his strength and pitch at that high level.

What many people may not know about Mr. "I'd rather be lucky than good" was that he and the Yankees management decided to have most of his teeth pulled, and then have him drink three quarts of milk each day. The Yankees also agreed to give him unlimited meal money each day. They were positive this would improve his strength. I don't know how the missing teeth and the milk were supposed to help, but these were the lengths he went to. More than likely, because Lefty played with the Yankees from 1930 to 1943, this was the medical science of the time (Alexander, 2002).

Even so, Lefty Gomez understood the value of doing whatever it takes to succeed. Luck is a contributing factor, but it's not nearly enough to round out a successful career.

Hard work is a part of the equation that's not talked about enough in my field, either. Some high-level musicians fail to mention the countless hours they spent in their youth sitting on their bed and practicing scales up and down the fret board while their buddies were out playing baseball or chasing girls. They forget about the times they were laughed or booed off stage because of the horrible band they were in at age 16, along with their also-16-year-old band mates. They never really talk about performing in three bands, working at Lowe's, and living on a friend's couch before something finally came together for them.

Instead, they are humble. And I get it.

No successful person wants to appear smug. Hubris isn't an attractive feature at all. Yet, somewhere along the way, we want to tip our cap to the work that goes into success. Nobody deserves success or a good paying job. You work toward it.

The language of praise from managers needs to incorporate this. Rather than use a term like deserve, focus on the work and effort that went into the achievement. Emphasize that the employee earned the recognition. The sweat of one's brow and the persistence of internal motivation should be identified and reinforced.

I get disheartened when I hear of employees whose accomplishments aren't recognized, or worse, ignored. They receive no acknowledgement from either peers or superiors when they do things well and in a timely manner. They feel management expects perfection and punishes anything short of it. For a moment, imagine being the employee in that situation. How would you feel? What would you do? An executive may expect perfection, but not everyone around will share this point of view. Empathize and respect the employees' perspective.

Help employees set goals. Achievement is born from the satisfaction of setting and accomplishing goals. For employees who enter the workforce without this ability, a good manager can help mentor and develop this skill. In no way is this meant to be demeaning; the ability to knock a goal out of the park isn't something we are born with. It isn't innate. It is learned over time. Management and team leads can step up and help employees create goals.

I often hear of executive and management staff feeling frustrated because they believe prospective employees entering the workforce lack direction. But change requires directed action. We can either sit around and complain about the younger generation (as I'm sure our parents and our parents' parents did with us), or we can figure out what to do about it.

Goal setting requires vision beyond the next week or two, but breaking down a long term goal into digestible and manageable steps is also a skill. Here is where transparency comes back into play. Managers who help employees understand the overall mission of the company can help the employee recognize where they fit in. Breaking down the long-term mission into the exact purpose of the individual employee can help them see where they fit in the larger picture.

Helping them see the progression of what they are doing to reach the larger goal can help them, not only in your company, but in their own life, too. Remember successive approximations—breaking a bigger goal into small steps. Little goals performed along the way are manageable and doable.

When you teach a dog to catch a Frisbee, you don't just whip the disc across an open field and expect the dog to run after it, leap into the air, and then snag it like an outfielder robbing the batter of a home run.

That would be absurd!

Likewise, you wouldn't toss the Frisbee at the dog while you're both sitting in your living room. It would probably bounce off their snout and fall harmlessly to the ground. Now the dog is confused, and you are frustrated.

Instead of expecting the dog to grasp the lofty expectation of snatching that flying disc out of the air, you start small and build the skill.

You start out with getting the dog to associate the toy with good things. Feed the dog out of the Frisbee, as if it were a dish, and they'll associate the toy with being fed. Play tug-of-war with the Frisbee. Just as with the food, the dog associates the Frisbee with the good feeling of play, along with all the inherent rewards of spending time with their owner. While playing, gently toss the Frisbee around. As it goes up and down, the dog will track the disc as it moves through the air.

Of course, I am in no way comparing your employees to dogs! What I want to do is show that immediately expecting people to fully grasp the exact nature of their mission may be too much at first. Go from big picture to small picture, complete with the requisite steps and reinforcements toward goal attainment. Grow their need for achievement. Make them feel like a part of a larger whole and create achievable goals toward that end. Help them understand the why behind the what.

One thing that needs to be clear is the concept of manageable (or doable). A main part of a manager's job is to always keep tabs on deadlines, quotas, and targets. A truly perceptive manager is also aware of the varying levels of motivation, skill, and drive among the employees. They know the right time to push and challenge their employees' mettle, and the right time to back away and give their employees room to breathe and relax. Remaining cognizant of the energy level of the workforce (mental, emotional, and physical) is critical to maintaining maximum output and creativity.

Here is where all those relationship skills come into play. Stay connected to the people who work for, and around, you. Instead of entering a room and demanding everyone orient toward you, enter a room, and take inventory of who is there and how they are doing.

The best managers are adaptive leaders; they know when to back off and let the team members create and make suggestions without fear of punishment. Conversely, they know when to step in and correct a situation using constructive criticism if they see a group moving in an undesirable direction. The adaptive leaders are the ones who know when to push the gas, and when to ease off the accelerator.

Notice I didn't say "hit the brake." Businesses can't operate with a foot on the brake. As the economic landscape continues to develop, competition is a constant in every industry. Therefore, easing off the accelerator to continue the forward momentum is how success perseveres.

Your employees have good days and bad days. They have fights with their spouse, they worry over sick children, they endure a flat tire on the way to the office. By the same token, they also enjoy the best cup of coffee they've ever had, just watched their child graduate with honors, or finally closed on the first home they have ever owned. Their lives don't slow down or cease to exist just because they are at work.

Remember, good things energize people, but those things also create a certain kind of stress. It's called "eustress" by psychology professionals, and it does affect focus, concentration, creativity, and dedication. The difference is that it does this in a positive way. A challenge where the goal doesn't seem impossible brings hope and engagement to a person. Being mindful of your employees helps you know when to hold 'em and when to fold 'em.

Your company will go through periods when everyone needs to put the hammer down and go full tilt. A huge order, a big audit, or an insanely busy time of year, such as Christmas shopping in retail establishments, require an "all hands on deck" approach. Those times, unfortunately, cannot be avoided. Management's challenge is to keep morale high while your employees are going that extra mile.

Outside of any anomalies, honesty and connectedness will separate good managers from subpar, and energize a workforce toward maximum production.

***

A good piece of business advice comes from the ancient Temple of Apollo in Central Greece. The advice is part of the 147 Delphic maxims, a bunch of proverbs and sayings that the ancient Greeks did their best to live by. Three of the maxims are carved above the entrance to the temple. Just so you don't feel that you have to travel there to read the words for yourself, I'll go ahead and tell you the one maxim I'm referring to: Medan Agan, or Nothing in Excess (Robertson, 2020). Or, to put it into more everyday language, too much of a good thing is still a bad thing. This holds very true for a certain kind of employee: the high achiever, one who will go beyond reasonable expectations to reach a high level of success.

At first, this may sound like a great thing. Is there such a thing as too much tenacity? What company wouldn't want a few deeply tenacious people who go above and beyond the requirements of every job? Contrary to what this may look like on the surface, an employee like this on a team can be more of a liability than an asset.

High achieving employees, like any other kind of employee, do not exist in a void. They're on "go" every moment they are on the job. As a result, they are often unaware how their exhausting activity affects everyone around them. They can incite professional envy, which is a very real problem in a team environment. High achieving employees are driven to work faster and take unnecessary risks. They demoralize their co-workers by insisting on perfection; if their impossible standards are not met, they become hypercritical, impatient, and intolerant of their fellow co-workers.

As you could imagine, employees who work at a normal, reasonable pace will not respond well to this treatment. They give their driven co-worker condescending looks, exclusion from office gatherings, and bad peer reviews. Or, if frustrated enough, they may simply bark back with, "Hey, slow down!"

Employees relate to each other in ways like siblings in a family. Rivalry, competition for resources, attention-seeking behavior, and envy become very evident. Depending upon the different background and behaviors of the employees, they will have learned different strategies to get their needs met in the group, often at the expense of the high achiever. Obviously, there is no way to know this could happen ahead of time, but a manager can anticipate problems and generate solutions ahead of a crisis.

For the time being, give the high achieving employee some tools to use among their peer group. Management can let them know that their true strengths are appreciated—no one can be an expert in everything. Help them prioritize their goals—being productive is far better than being busy. Let them know that mistakes are not critical failures but are simply lessons to learn.

As far as the rest of the team, help manage their perceptions about the high achiever. Rather than slow down your fastest racehorse, allow the others to keep up. Allow the others to see how accurate, creative, and effective work is acknowledged and rewarded by your management staff. Good will can be spread around the company to inspire all workers without showing favoritism.

Chapter 11: Overcoming Adversity

The flexibility and tenacity required to overcome adversity is paramount to success. In fact, I coach people to expect adversity so they can formulate an action plan to overcome. Understanding adversity as a concept forms the foundation to overcome it.

I myself have managed to face adversity by walking through the fire.

***

I like to remain positive in life. My metaphor of treating the future like an unopened Christmas present is also how I approach decisions and opportunities. Not everything comes out smelling like a rose—there are adversities in life. If we treat them as bricks instead brick walls, we can maneuver around them and look for alternative opportunities, even if we stub our toes on the way past them.

When a window closes, a door opens, right?

However, my positivity isn't perfect. Don't think for a minute that I am above feeling hurt, betrayed, or angry. I'm human like everyone else, and sometimes I have to consciously pull myself out of those pits that we all fall into from time to time.

The idea here is not about avoiding adversity—it's about how you handle it and how you recover.

***

It was 1984, close to the end of Cyndi Lauper's She's So Unusual Tour.

On a major tour, life gets routine. We travel, we sleep, we hit sound check, we meet the fans, we perform, and we travel.

Lather, rinse, repeat.

We do have days off and time to relax, but the routine pretty much stays the same. Occasionally, the artist hits a milestone (for example, a million in album sales or a single hitting number one) and celebrates with the band. With the success of Cyndi's debut album, we had those champagne meetings often.

Toward the end of the tour, Cyndi called everyone together for a band meeting in her hotel room. She had Platinum Status and was looking forward to keeping the momentum going in the future. Plus,

Cyndi improvising with me

she was (and still is) an enormously generous and kind person, so she wanted to begin sharing her success with the people on stage who support her every night.

She called the meeting to order and talked about what she had in mind.

"When this tour is over, I want all of you to play on the next record. I love what you guys do. You helped me sell five million records so far. I want to keep you guys and make you a full-time band."

Further, she told us we were welcome to contribute songs, which would have meant a nice financial payoff if any made the second album. She also said the band would have a name. Think Joan Jett and the Blackhearts or George Thorogood and the Delaware Destroyers, or Bruce Springsteen and the East Street Band.

As a part of having a name, she was going to give us our own merchandise deal. In my mind, I could see our t-shirts selling alongside Cyndi's in the merch tent. It was a little overwhelming to digest, truth be told.

Little did we know, she saved the best for last.

"...and you guys are all going to get a point on the next record."

Giving a "point" means you are granting a band member a percentage of the album's profits. I'm not an expert on the accounting end of things, but my understanding is that every point on a platinum-selling album (one million copies) is worth about $200,000.

Her first album sold six million copies, and her follow-up LP was slated to do even better.

The enormity of it all! We were going to be her band. We were able to contribute songs. We were getting a unique name and a merchandising deal. We were going to each get a point on the follow-up album. And we were still going to get paid for every tour date and every recording session. This was huge news! We started this gig as salaried sidemen, and now we were faced with the possibility of being partners and shareholders in a multi-platinum record that had yet to be recorded.

The band went down to the hotel bar. Beers were flowing while we talked about the future. We were flying high! A bunch of sidemen were about to get the keys to the kingdom.

Fast forward to early 1986—the time between Cyndi's albums when I connected with the band Craaft. I had already agreed to do the European tour where they opened for Queen. I was having a great time. While on that tour, I received a phone call from Cyndi's road manager, Robin Irvine. We were in Germany, and I was sound asleep when I answered the call.

He said, "Hey Sandy...are you sitting down?"

"Yeah. There's a six-hour time difference here, Robin. I'm sleeping. What's up?"

I wasn't prepared for his answer.

"Cyndi fired the whole band."

I jumped to my feet. "What?! Why?"

I learned that Cyndi had parted ways with her manager, David Wolff. Dave in the Doorway was not only her manager, he was also romantically involved with her. Their personal breakup was painful for Cyndi (and Dave, for that matter), so when she ended the romantic relationship, she also broke up with him professionally. The band, who had all been hired by David, would have been a nagging reminder of Dave to Cyndi. She wanted to spare herself the heartache, so she cleaned house altogether.

Robin went out of his way to assure me it was nothing personal. It wasn't just me. The entire band was out. Not that it cushioned the blow.

I have to admit, I was bitter about it for quite a while afterward. It was a huge disappointment. There was a period when I really wasn't sure how I would act if I ever ran into Cyndi again. Sure, it was "'just business," but I was left feeling very disappointed.

Time marched on. I ran into her a few times in the early 1990s. We came face-to-face and exchanged some chit-chat. The one thing that impressed me most was how warm she was toward me. She was the old Cyndi Lauper I remembered. No animosity came from her end.

That helped me relax and let the disappointment fade.

The Davy Jones concert in Dallas happened after the big breakup. I felt comfortable calling and inviting her to make a surprise appearance with Davy that night because I knew we were good. I had let bygones be bygones. I looked at her as a positive in my life; she was the reason I had achieved so much. She was the reason for all I had, rather than the reason for anything I didn't have.

Cyndi and I hung out for quite a while after the Davy Jones/Dallas show. She opened up to me in a way she never had when I was her employee. I learned a lot of things I had never known. She gave me the chance to understand her point of view.

When she let the band go in 1986, I realized I had never considered her point of view. That was on me. From that point on, I always remembered that moment in the bar with her and how a five-minute conversation cleared up many years of hard feelings that still lingered.

The greatest lesson I learned, though, was that there's always another point of view.

Cyndi Lauper with my family, 2018

Conversations are two-way streets. I strive to be a good listener and an understanding person. Moments like this keep me honest and demonstrate how life and relationships are a constant learning process.

If we're lucky, we grow by sips every day and by gulps during critical moments.

The last time I saw Cyndi, it was like seeing family. In 2018, she opened for Rod Stewart at the Bridgestone Arena in Nashville. I took my then-24-year-old daughter to see the show, and Cyndi was kind enough to invite us backstage.

She hugged me, hugged my daughter, and acted like we didn't miss a stitch. Everything was just as warm as it had always been. All anyone needs to know about Cyndi Lauper is that I would go to the end of the world for her.

***

Getting fired by Cyndi was a bitter pill to swallow for a few reasons. Many expectations were yanked out from under me (the financial one was the most difficult). There's a life lesson here in and of itself: Expectation leads to disappointment. Do your best to accept the future on the future's terms rather than try to force it into your terms.

Also, I was close to Cyndi and felt like I was betrayed by a friend.

The entire event—from the decision to the execution—was completely out of my control. I had no power to control the outcome, and that felt awful.

Screwing up the Rod Stewart audition was an equally bitter pill for me, but for an entirely different reason. That time, it was completely my fault. That should have given me some sensible perspective, but honestly, that just made it so much worse. Second-guessing and beating myself up for the mistake were all I did for a couple weeks after the audition.

It took a while before I could even function well enough to persevere. I landed on my feet, but it took tremendous tenacity…and Carmine Appice.

Once I got home from the Rod Stewart audition, I didn't know what to do. I cried myself to sleep that night. I really did. I was living in Los Angeles, 3,000 miles from my home and family in New York—although it might well have been a million miles. On top of that, my first marriage was falling apart. I felt like a big, sad polar bear, floating on an ice shelf, adrift and disconnected from hope. My drinking escalated significantly. And I had the worst insomnia I've ever had in my life.

I called my mother and cried to her on the phone. She was concerned, like any mom would be. Thankfully, I didn't feel suicidal through any of this, but that didn't cross my mother's mind. What truly concerned her was that I was in substantial pain, and as a mom, she felt her child's pain, too.

I prayed to God every night. I didn't know where to turn. I was broke, alone, and desperate. I needed something; anything to hang my hat on and reverse the downward spiral.

Then, one day, I found I had had enough. I hit my breaking point. I collected myself, and I decided I would not give up on music. Who knows why or how I came to that decision. Maybe it was a little wink from God. I'll probably never know. But I dusted myself off and went to the local library.

I got a reference book published annually by Billboard magazine called the Billboard International Talent & Touring Directory. It lists every manager in the music industry, and every band they work with. The list is cross-referenced with all the bands listed alphabetically, so you can search by your favorite band name or by the manager's name.

Because it was a reference book, I couldn't check it out of the library. So, I brought in a legal pad and wrote down the names and addresses of 50 managers who oversaw the bands I really liked. I began to put together my resume, but it was missing one important thing: a good reference.

During my two and a half years in Los Angeles, Carmine Appice had seen me play a handful of times. In addition to his presence being an honor, it was also a key component in my last gasp at making it in Los Angeles. I needed a high-profile reference, and Carmine was the guy.

I ran into him during a rehearsal at SIR and asked face to face if I could use him as a reference. He agreed—no big deal. It became the only noteworthy reference on my resume, and his name and number proved to be critical.

I now had a complete resume. I stapled a photo of me playing the drums to all 50 mimeographed copies of the resume. I sent the 50 resumes to the 50 managers.

And I waited.

And waited....

...and waited.

I never heard back from a single person, except one. I sent one resume to Peter Grant, manager of Led Zeppelin. He lived in England, but all his mail went to Swan Song Records on Madison Avenue in New York. However, Peter wasn't the guy who saw the resume at first. At Swan Song Records, Led Zeppelin's attorney, Steve Weiss, took it upon himself to open Peter Grant's mail.

He could have forwarded my sealed resume to England along with the rest of Peter Grant's mail, but he didn't. I have no idea why he decided to open that particular envelope on that particular day, but he tore mine open and took a look.

The synchronicity kicked in. My higher power, that universal force moved me ahead a few squares on the game board of life.

As it turned out, Steve Weiss himself was putting a band together. He was in the process of shopping some songs written by a couple of unknowns named Michael Bolotin (who later adopted the stage name Michael Bolton) and Bruce Kulick.

If you aren't familiar with Bruce's name, he is quite a big deal in rock and roll. His big break came when he and his brother, Bob, toured for Meatloaf's Bat Out of Hell tour in 1977, both sharing duties as rhythm and lead guitarists. Bruce became a member of the band Kiss in 1984, replacing original member Ace Frehley. He held that post for twelve years, leaving only because Ace returned to the band in 1996. Bruce is currently the lead guitarist for Grand Funk Railroad, and has been since 2000. In my humble opinion, Bruce is a gifted guitar player.

Steve Weiss had used a session bass player and a session drummer on the demos, so they needed to hire full-time players to fill out the band. This meant Steve needed a bass player and a drummer. Pronto!

A turn of events occurred that I seriously believe was an act of Divine Intervention. Guess whose resume just happened to show up at that very moment? Furthermore, he opened a resume that wasn't even addressed to him.

He looked over my resume and saw that I lived in Los Angeles. That was unfortunate; Steve wanted a New York guy to work with. For some reason, he turned to page two of my resume before throwing it in the trash—and saw Carmine Appice's name as one of my references!

Hope you're sitting down for the next one.

Steve Weiss used to be the attorney for Vanilla Fudge, of which Carmine was a member. Steve knew Carmine extremely well, and he took this opportunity to give Carmine a call. If for no other reason, he would at least enjoy catching up with his old friend. But he also wanted the lowdown on this kid named Sandy Gennaro.

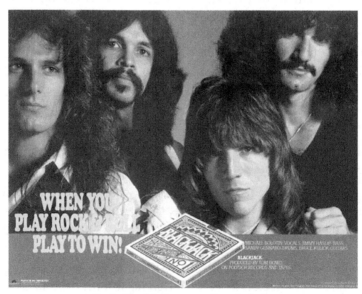

Early Blackjack promotional photo

Carmine vouched for me. I knew he would, which is why it was important to me that he be listed as a reference. Even more so, Carmine informed Steve that I was a New York guy, born and bred. I just happened to live in Los Angeles at the time.

Steve called me. "Hi, Sandy. You sent a resume to Peter Grant. It ended up in the mail tray here at Swan Song Records. I'm Steve Weiss, the attorney for Led Zeppelin."

I listened, my head spinning. He continued. "Carmine vouched for you. I'm looking for a drummer for a new project. Would you be willing to fly to New York to audition for this band?"

"Oh, hell yeah! When?"

He sent a prepaid ticket.

I flew to New York and stayed at my mother's house on Staten Island. I auditioned on a Wednesday, got called back that Friday, and played the audition songs again—only with a different bass player. The new guy was Jimmy Haslip, who got the gig with me.

Michael and Bruce loved the rhythm section and signed on with the new band, Blackjack. A couple weeks and a few rehearsals later, we did a showcase for several record labels. PolyGram Records won the bid. We were officially signed to a subsidiary label called Polydor.

When I flew back to Los Angeles, I had a contract for a seven-record deal with two guaranteed in my back pocket. Not long after that, I returned to live in New York, triumphant and renewed.

Blackjack had the record deal, but we had to figure out who was going to produce the initial album. Steve set up an audition with a legendary producer.

***

Tom Dowd didn't produce new bands. At this point in his career, he didn't need to. But he agreed to produce Blackjack.

Tom Dowd is deeply important to me because a lot of my management (and drumming) style comes directly from what I learned interacting with Tom. He was a brilliant producer, overseeing many legendary performers in several genres. He engineered and produced projects in the R&B genre for hall of fame artists Ray Charles, The Drifters, The Coasters, and The Spinners. He worked with jazz prodigies John Coltrane, Thelonious Monk, and Charlie Parker. He guided rock and roll royalty like Eric Clapton, The Eagles, The Allman Brothers, and Chicago. I would list his complete resume, but it would take up this entire book. This man was an innovator and a giant in the field.

The great Tom Dowd

He also had a way of understanding and connecting with people that I have rarely seen before or since. He could salve the bruised egos of temperamental artists, motivate the discouraged, and keep a band focused and productive through the most trying of times. Living in a recording studio for five or six weeks is a grind. It can try the patience of young artists who aren't blessed with patience or diplomacy.

I learned a tremendous amount about the psychology of a producer from Tom. Music producers (who are the managers of the music industry) can get results without acting like a dictator. With grace and wisdom, Tom demonstrated to me how he got results.

It was one of those many days in the studio when we worked on the Blackjack album. That day, we weren't recording using a click track or a metronome. We recorded the songs live, meaning we played them in the studio with microphones set up around my drums to record the live performance directly. At one point during a song, Tom stopped us.

Quietly, he took me aside to talk. He started with, "Sandy, you're going to do great things behind the drum set. You're going to play with a lot of famous people and do quite well in the music business."

"But Sandy…what I want to know is: why did you play a four-beat fill there?"

What I had played was a one-measure fill to introduce the chorus. Not a big deal. "Well," I said, "I thought it was a really good fill."

Tom thought for a moment, "I thought it was a good fill, too. But that's not the question I asked you. I asked why you played a long fill there."

I had no answer for him, so he continued.

"Listen, it really was a great fill. It was well-executed, but it didn't fit the song. Save that fill for your clinics or for your drum solo. If a fill doesn't fit the song, save it. Play for the song. Serve the song."

This was Tom's philosophy for rock and roll drumming. Contrary to what some people may think regarding rock rhythms, less is more. No need to be an "all icing" guy. Be a "cake" guy. Just do something simple to alert the listener to changes or separations in differing sections of the music.

Tom continued. "Did you ever think about practicing with a metronome?"

Tom was also the first person to teach me how to properly use a metronome. I had never done that before, as crazy as it sounds. For drummers in particular, a metronome is a very critical tool and instructional aide. Our entire purpose is to keep time and internalizing the click of the metronome makes us better at our job.

Sure, I could have stewed on his question and recognized it as rhetorical. After all, what else could I say in that moment? I could have twisted it into feeling that I had failed and that he was being condescending or critical. But it would have been hard to do that because he was so open and caring with his words.

Underneath his words was a very clear sentiment: He was trying to improve my time keeping. He was trying to make me better because he thought I could do great things.

I was eager to take his advice. This was Tom Dowd. Who else better to glean some pearls of wisdom? I take a position to learn from those who know more than me or are better at something than me.

He sent me to a friend of his who owned a music store and told me which metronome to get. I bought it and began to practice that very afternoon.

Tom gave advice in a very unique way. His message was solid, but it was the way he said it. He framed his feedback in a positive direction. He heard something in my playing that showed I wasn't as good at keeping time as I thought I was. I wasn't bad, but I probably lacked the consistency he was looking for. Instead of calling me out in front of everyone ("Sandy! Your timing sucks!"), he pulled me aside to talk.

He built me up first. He made me feel good so I would continue to listen. I respected what he said. This also showed me that whatever came next, Tom was not trying to tear me down or take away from any

137

Taking a break with Tom Dowd

of my current skills. He demonstrated that he was impressed and only trying to make me better. That's an important delineation for CEOs, managers, parents, and anyone else in a position of authority. Support and build rather than tear down and destroy.

He liked the fill; he agreed it was indeed a good fill. But he corrected me only after he told me what made it good. He made sure I could hear and understand his direction because I wasn't defending my honor, my ability, or my point of view. I relaxed, listened, and respected his feedback.

His delivery was as smooth as he could have offered. He didn't dictate or order me to do anything. There was no "edict" I could be hurt with, so nothing to rebel or push against. He obviously thought I could benefit from practicing with a metronome but wanted to make it my idea rather than his idea. He planted a seed.

Clear message + simple instruction + effective delivery = positive results.

When I manage and lead people, I always think about Tom Dowd. Build people up; it'll create an atmosphere of better performance over time.

The invisible hand of Divinity intervened again. I had contemplated giving up music to find a steady, full-time, nine-to-five job. Then I found myself at Criteria Studios in Miami with Tom Dowd, the guy in the liner notes of so many beloved albums.

I was as happy as a lark. I overcame adversity.

***

As a side guy or a session musician, my role would have ended once the basic tracks for the Blackjack album were complete. By basic tracks, I mean the foundation or rhythm section of a song, usually bass and drums. Because I was an actual member of the band Blackjack, I didn't have to leave once the basic tracks were done. I got to be a fly on the wall. I had the opportunity to sit in the control room for the remainder of the production to experience the overdubs, vocals, mixing, and other aspects. I'd soak in everything I saw or heard Tom do and say.

It came time for Bruce Kulick to go into the studio and come up with an intro to the song "Love Me Tonight," which also became our first single off the album. Therefore, Tom understood the importance of that single having a good intro.

As Bruce was tuning his guitar in the studio, I overheard Tom talking to the engineer in the control room, out of Bruce's earshot. "Hey...I'm thinking of this for the intro." Tom "sang" a few bars of music he wanted Bruce to play to the engineer.

Next, Tom punched the in-studio mic and said into it, "Hey Bruce...we need an intro for the song. Whaddya got?"

Any other producer who was more of a Boss than a Leader might have punched the in-studio mic and said, "Hey Bruce! Play this!" He would then sing the bars he wanted to hear for the intro. But Tom is not a Boss; he's an adaptive Leader. He doesn't dictate; he allows the creative atmosphere to build on its own terms, and with creative people in his crew. What Tom did and said was something very different, but far more effective.

He asked Bruce to come up with some ideas for the intro, which Bruce did.

This is a complex endeavor for the guitar players. On almost every rock and roll album you hear, the intros, fills, and solos are crafted almost on the spot by the guitarists. Ask any of them how they came

139

up with a riff, and they'll usually not give a straightforward answer. Honestly, I don't think they're quite sure themselves. They open the creative side of their mind and see what flows out of their hands. Sometimes they nail it in one take, other times they have to noodle around a bit before arriving on the answer they're looking for.

From a producer's standpoint, this haphazard process can try their patience. They're trying to move things along to complete the album by the deadline given to them from their manager. The yin and yang of giving the artist rope, versus telling them what to do, is a struggle that each producer resolves in a way that suits his or her style. For Tom Dowd, his resolution was to build Bruce Kulick up and make him feel that the finished product was all his idea instead of Tom's. That gave Bruce a sense of satisfaction as an artist, a feeling of ownership over the song, and the reinforcement of knowing he made Tom proud and happy. The strategy was brilliant.

The whole collaboration took about fifteen minutes of back and forth. Bruce would play a few licks, then Tom would shape Bruce's ideas until it morphed into what he originally sang to the engineer. I was fascinated as I watched it unfold.

Bruce came up with a lick.

Tom would encourage him to try something different. "You're getting warmer, Bruce!"

Bruce changed it up slightly.

"Oh! I liked that change. Let's keep working. I think it's getting hot."

Bruce added a few good notes and took away a few bad notes.

"Bruce, seriously…I think you're almost there. This is really good."

This time, Bruce would make slight changes until the sound was close to what Tom originally sang out.

"Excellent, Bruce! That was brilliant! Don't change a thing! You just came up with a fantastic into."

I love Bruce, so I feel comfortable mentioning that he can be a little neurotic at times. But when he heard those words from Tom, I could physically see Bruce light up and lift his head a little higher. "Thanks, Tommy!"

All Tom Dowd did was tell Bruce he did a good job, but that was huge for Bruce. A profound sense of satisfaction and pride was reflected in every ounce of his body language when he walked out of the studio. Plus, now every time Bruce puts on that record for his friends, he can say, "I came up with that!"

The process was fun to watch, but even more fun to apply in my personal life.

***

To overcome adversity, we first have to agree that adversity is an inevitable part of life. The phrase "nothing ventured, nothing gained" applies here, as it suggests that without risk there can be no reward. It's a risk to open a business. It's a risk to grow your business. It's a risk to get married, or start a family, or purchase a home. If you insulate yourself from all possible risk, your life would be as exciting as unflavored gelatin.

Sure, some people might say "...as exciting as vanilla ice cream." Fun fact: real vanilla, from a real vanilla orchid bean, is the best, most complex flavor you will ever put in your mouth. And that is why vanilla ice cream is the best. End of that story—back to adversity.

Each time you face and overcome adversity, you grow a little stronger. Maybe not to the extreme of "whatever doesn't kill you makes you stronger," but overcoming challenges allows us to see ourselves as resilient and resourceful. We learn that we can take a blow and still stay upright, thus enhancing our confidence to overcome future adversity!

Screwing up the Rod Stewart audition and getting fired by Cyndi Lauper were two huge blows in my life. I landed on my feet, but it certainly didn't feel that way at the time. I had to take time to absorb the blow and move on. I didn't have an actual strategy back then, but I can break it down now to better understand why I chose the path I did back then.

We can all probably agree that the most certain thing in life is uncertainty. Most aspects of our lives are completely out of our control, despite our best efforts.

One of the biggest certainties we face as humans is our mortality—we all know we will die one day. Being self-aware of our mortality affects how we think and act in our daily life. For many people, it can create deep feelings of dread and anxiety.

To artificially create a sense of control over their fear of death, they may indulge in one of a huge range of self-destructive behaviors. For example, they might drink too much, do drugs, or eat terribly.

Of course, those who engage in any self-destructive or death-defying behavior will still die one day. Those behaviors do not help control this aspect of life.

So, rather than fight to control the inevitable, let's shift our mindset to accept the inevitable, and deal with it accordingly.

When adversity strikes (and it will), the first order of business is to prepare for all possible outcomes, including the negative ones. Anticipate things going wrong and make a plan to overcome or deal with them. Ask yourself: What is the worst thing that can happen? Ask realistically because the next step is to react as if the worst thing has happened.

What do you do? Break it down into steps. Construct a plan. Then, construct a solid backup plan if the first plan goes haywire. Doing so can help you to feel confident and prepared. If everything goes sideways, you will not have to think on your feet. You've got it covered.

You obviously can't anticipate everything that could possibly go wrong, but planned adversity creates a "forewarned is forearmed" mentality.

When something you didn't expect happens, choose how you respond to the event. You can interpret it as the worst thing that could ever happen, believe you will never recover from it, and take from it that bad things always happen to you because you are cursed.

Or look at the event as neither positive nor negative. Yes, consequences exist. I'm not foolish enough to think everything is going to be wonderful in the aftermath. But I will create a new mindset, an internal narrative of belief in a positive outcome. We cannot predict our future; we do not know what, if anything, is in store for us. If something awful happens today, it could be the catalyst that brings something great the next day. Open yourself to the possibility of positivity and proceed when you see the opportunity arise.

As you assess your expectations, calibrate them to reflect reality. Frame them in a positive light by creating a positive expectancy. As we all know, reality can bring both positive and negative results to us. And that we cannot control—but we can control how we see it.

I once heard a speaker say, "Expectation creates disappointment." That simple phrase really stuck with me. It pushes us to pigeonhole our expectations into a place of gloom, despair, and pessimism. Again, reality isn't always negative!

I would love for Cyndi's promise to have come true! But that was out of my control. For all I know, it may not have ended up the way I anticipated. Was it disappointing to lose that gig? Absolutely! Will it be the end of me as an entertainer and professional musician? Absolutely not!

Talk yourself through handling the outcome. Getting fired by Cyndi didn't change who I was as a person. It didn't blackball me from working with any other artists. It didn't make my family love me or support me less. Rather, it was a temporary setback to my financial situation, and it forced me to get creative and find a new gig. Nothing more, nothing less.

I will stand by my conviction. Every setback is both a temporary setback and a learning experience. There are stories of people all over the world who have experienced extreme adversity, and yet, they came out on top. They turned their setback into inner strength and resolve to overcome the obstacle. I don't have the market cornered on overcoming adversity, but I have taken my blows and am still here before you.

Shore up your external resources. This isn't about money—I'm referring to something greater. Make sure you cultivate your support system! Your friends, your family, your significant other; whoever will be in your corner when life has you against the ropes. Not that person who'll throw in the towel on your behalf. I'm talking about the one who'll splash water on your face and tell you to keep going—even when you think you can't.

Finally, take action. Sure, it's standard advice, but I can't stress it enough. When the world is moving against you, plan a move and execute, if for no other reason than to gain a small victory. Sometimes you just need a win. By acting, you stand a better chance of being instrumental in turning things around. Sitting still only allows your mind to continue churning in a pit of negativity. Rather than ruminate, take the bull by the horns and get started creating your own breaks.

One of the biggest challenges I faced when I screwed up the Rod Stewart audition was the isolation I felt living in Los Angeles. I and my wife at the time had grown apart due to a lot of strife within the marriage. My family felt a million miles away on the East Coast, and I was too embarrassed and wounded to talk to my friends. Over time, I ditched my destructive habits and activated my support network. My friends all helped me vent my frustration constructively.

Carmine Appice was the friend who spring-boarded me into the band Blackjack. In addition to Carmine, there were a handful of other good friends who lent their support and strength when I allowed them into my misery.

That led me to mimeographing and mailing out those 50 resumes. I couldn't create my own break without the help of Carmine and a little bit of divine intervention. However, like playing the lottery, I would have never won had I never played. I made the decision to move on. I shored up my network and took swift, directed action. The adversity still lingered in the background, but I didn't let it keep me down for long.

When I was let go by Cyndi Lauper, the biggest challenge I faced was overcoming my internal reaction of severe disappointment. I was in a much different place professionally than when I auditioned for Rod Stewart—I wasn't considering packing it all in and tossing my drumsticks into the Hudson River. But I was still very disappointed. The emotional piece was a difficult hurdle for me, as I am sure you can imagine.

When it comes to lessening the emotional impact, I would like to share a passage I read in a column written by a personal development expert named Cephas Tope. He wrote a short column titled "5 Ways to Deal with Adversity in Life." This simple sentence has stuck with me because it was jarringly accurate:

You can't get ahead in life while you're trying to get even (Tope, n.d.).

Truthful, don't you think? Resentment requires a lot of mental energy, and it can distract you from focusing on the important things that move you forward. If you carry an ulterior motive, then you may miss opportunities because you are not open to positive outcomes in your own life. Remember: your resentment does not hurt the other person at all. They may be aware of your hard feelings but are probably moving on and forging a new path for themselves.

In all honesty, nobody likes to be around a negative, resentful person. That attitude will bleed into conversations and strategy sessions. You may think you're hiding it from the rest of the world, but people around you will still pick up on it. Even if not overtly expressed, the undercurrent will be obvious. Negativity breeds negativity.

Mr. Tope ends his column with a somewhat altered Biblical quote from Galatians, 6:17:

From henceforth let nothing trouble me,
for I bear in my mind the mark of forgiveness.

If someone has wronged you, do yourself a favor and forgive. Move on.

If you are the one who has wronged yourself (like me with Rod Stewart), take a moment to forgive yourself and move on. Living in the past is distracting from the wondrous possibilities of the present.

Chapter 12: Energy

I would be remiss to not acknowledge that both tenacity and overcoming adversity require a tremendous amount of energy to accomplish. When I use the word "energy" here, I'm not referring to physics. I'm talking about the motivation and capacity a person has to take action.

Successful people don't necessarily have an endless fountain of energy inherent to their nature. Some are quiet, pensive, introverted, or unassuming. No one single personality rises to the top. Instead, successful people maximize the energy they have.

Some successful people maintain their energy through practicing healthy physical and mental habits. Sleep, diet, and exercise are touted as the holy trinity of health. Being fit above and below the neck will both boost and maintain your energy. This is a critical concept that cannot be ignored if you endeavor to be successful.

***

The prime motivator for all of us is the pursuit of happiness. It helps narrow a person's focus on what is important to them, thus they know where to direct their energy. Having a clearly defined set of goals can aid in directing energy, too.

So, how does happiness pertain to managers and employees? What if the things that make them happy don't line up with the mission of the company? Do you have to redefine for them what makes them happy? No. That's what a Boss would do–a Leader does not force an ideology onto their employee. Instead, they work with it.

This is an important discussion that managers will inevitably have with employees when the time comes for the Raise and Review process. Not only are previous accomplishments discussed, but goals for the future are considered for both the employee and the company.

Employees may possess goals that are external to the company— and that's a good thing! Any employee's goal can align with the company's mission. The key is showing this to the employee. Use their goal as a starting point and build a broader cognitive structure that includes your company.

Here is a possible scenario of an employee's Raise and Review discussion that begins with the employee giving a goal they may have.

"I just want to make enough money to buy a car."

"A new car? I can certainly understand that. You have a good, reasonable objective to reach for."

Some large companies have loan programs and special savings accounts that the manager can bring up to the employee. If the employee shows interest, the manager can point the employee to Human Resources; that kind of information is what they provide.

The manager can reinforce the goal for the employee at this point. "I know you can do it, and this company can get you there."

"Really? How?" asks the employee.

"Easy. Just...stick with us! Continue doing a great job with your duties as a (job title). When you do well, you are instantly a part of this company's success. And when the company succeeds, so do you! Our goal going forward is to get this (product/service) out to our customers. Help us take care of that and we will take care of you."

A concise conversation without judgment, criticism, or condescension will go a long way. Accept the employee where they are and help them see themselves inside the bigger picture. If you ignore what is important to them by forcing them to accept your goals as their own, you minimize the odds of success. Connect the two as if they are one goal and not mutually exclusive. Teach the why and the how behind the what.

You are expanding their awareness to include virtue, demonstrate the value of doing their work well, and helping them dispel the dread of setting an alarm clock each night before the next workday.

Feeling interconnected is the key to effective management. Will every employee respond and get immediately on board? No. That's not how all employees behave. Some may benefit from repetition of the message. Some may find their career path goes elsewhere. Don't stop doing the right thing because a handful of employees resist change. Build and create success in those who are ready to hear the message and take it to heart.

***

In his seminal work, Nicomachean Ethics, Aristotle defines happiness as living a life of virtue, acting according to rational intentionality, and performing tasks in accord with appropriate excellence. In other words, be a good person who treats others well, separate thought from action (act according to good decisions) and strive to always put forth your best work.

Those are the lessons I have been teaching in my live seminars and throughout this book. Until I did a little digging, I had no idea I was emulating Aristotle (it's probably too late to claim he stole these ideas from me). It is striking how basic the ideology can be. Productivity, intentionality, altruism, and happiness are inherently intertwined.

Further, Aristotle went on to philosophize about purpose. The purpose of every action we choose moves us toward a predicted happiness. Those same actions and decisions we make is in pursuit of general happiness. To demonstrate this, he challenged the reader to think of something they had done during the previous day. It didn't matter how mundane the activity; he simply instructed the reader to bring a specific activity to mind.

Then, he instructs the reader to ask themselves why they did that particular activity. Once they had an answer, he asks another "Why?"-based question (e.g.: "Why is _____ important to you?"). He continues to ask, "Why," to each consecutive answer, until the reader is funneled down to an answer that can no longer be challenged by the question "Why?"

This answer—the one that stands on its own merit—is theoretically the factor that motivates all human behavior. Aristotle felt it is the common denominator that motivates everything we do: "So I can be happy."

Let's look at how this works. Take the most basic activity that all of you currently have in common. You are either reading or listening to this book. Let's take that simple, shared activity and run it through Aristotle's questions of why. These may not be your answers; these answers are just an example.

Q: Why are you reading this book?

A: So I can learn how to be a more effective person (manager, employee, CEO, parent)

Q: Why is it important to you to be a better manager?

A: So I can do better work and make my company succeed.

Q: Why is it important for you to help your company succeed?

A: So we can make more money and maybe get a promotion.

Q: Why is it important to get promoted and make more money?

A: So I can afford to give my kids the life I never had.

Q: Why is it important to give your kids the life you never had?

A: So they grow up happy.

Q: Why do you want your kids to grow up happy?

A: So I feel like a good parent.

Q: Why do you want to feel like a good parent?

A: Because that will make me feel fulfilled; I'll feel happy.

For those of you who are a little more familiar with philosophy, you'll see that this method of Q & A is very much like the cooperative argumentative method that Socrates used in his teachings, a.k.a., Socratic method. What I show here is a very simplified version—Socrates' questions were far more open-ended to urge the student to think of new ideas, point out faulty presuppositions, and eliminate contradictions and hypocrisy. His method was not used to lead the student to one single, closed answer.

I'm not arrogant enough to think this book will lead a direct line to a better life, internal peace, and satisfaction for all. However, I am hoping readers will not ignore the contents of this book as they throw it on a shelf after they've waited in line to get it autographed. I really want to make a difference in your life because that would make me feel happy and fulfilled.

The exercise above doesn't only show that the prime motivator for all of us is the pursuit of happiness. It also helps to narrow a person's focus on what is important. Having a clearly defined set of goals can aid in moving energy in the right directions.

As you read the answers to the questions, you'll see that parenting comes up. For those who have children, they may not realize that being a good parent is so important on a very intimate level. At first, the questions follow a treadmill of working, traveling, and building a company. At the same time, they try to be a better parent than the absent parent was to them. When the dust settled, that clarity leads to some life changes, allowing the person to be more present at home. They become the good parent their mother or father never was; they give their kids the life they so dearly missed. Money is important to provide the necessities, of course—but clarity of goal and purpose is critical when allocating energy.

Some executives reading this may be wondering about happiness as it pertains to their managers and employees. What if the things that make them happy don't line up with the mission of the company? Do you have to redefine for them what makes them happy?

The answer is a firm No. That is what an autocratic Boss does—they tell people what to think. A Leader works with the happiness of the people, not against it. By honestly comparing the missions of both groups, you'll find that the company, as well as its employees, all seek happiness in the end.

Helping build a positive mindset is conducive to creating energy. Energy is a critical component of performance, as any athlete, musician, or certified public accountant will attest. As a executive or manager, your performance is clearly affected by your energy level. We have all had days where we felt depleted. Even high achievers have days where they feel exhausted.

How do we cultivate a positive energy flow in ourselves and share that spirit with our employees?

Honestly, it's not rocket science. It is not some new-age approach that will enlighten you or a scam devised to irritate you. All that's required is some good, old-fashioned common sense.

Let's revisit the "B" of BEATS: Belief. This refers to the belief in your employees and in your business. The concept is that belief creates positivity. Positivity is contagious; it will spread to every level, especially if your management staff is connected to the belief.

On a personal level, a belief in a higher power can help understand connectiveness. This has little to do with any one organized religion. If you can see the interconnectedness of all things and believe that the positivity you generate will be returned to you, then you are free to be spontaneous, caring, and altruistic.

These are mindsets that create and share positive energy. An altruistic person knows the forces that bind us all will pay them back for their good behavior, so they are motivated to give as much as possible. Other people feed off that energy, and it lifts up the entire group.

This also applies to overall health, both mental and physical. This is your belief in yourself. You have self-efficacy, the confidence that you can take care of things. That also includes taking care of yourself.

A healthy lifestyle should be encouraged among all staff within an organization. One role of management is to model appropriate corporate behavior to the employees. Management, from C-Level down to supervisors, should be coached in performing at consistently optimal levels of attitude, productivity, and ethics.

A healthy lifestyle also includes other themes presented in this book: kindness, positivity, and altruism. Striving toward exemplary mental health is critical to workplace relationships, disposition, creativity, and overall productivity. At a base level, the human organism relies on physical health to maintain life.

You already know of the benefit of a consistent regimen of exercise. In grade school, you were shown the importance of a healthy diet through the USDA Food Guide Pyramid (which became MyPlate in 2011). Many scientific sleep studies have shown how important sleep is to mental and physical health. You and your employees should know all of this—so what keeps people from actually doing what they already know will help them?

Let's be honest with ourselves for a moment. Living a healthy lifestyle is hard. It requires a lot of effort to make the sometimes-inconvenient choices required. But just because something is hard doesn't mean it's impossible. It just takes an open mind and some new strategies.

One reason some people give is "I just don't have the time." Of course, if you do nothing but wait for the right time to make a change, you're never going to change. Time must be made, not found. For example, incorporating exercise into your routine doesn't mean carving out an enormous crater of time every single day. Three days per week of moderate exercise (like, walking for 20-30 minutes) can have enormous mental and physical benefit (Chan, et al., 2018).

Can a busy person find that amount of time in a week to better their health? It is within the realm of possibility. Try trading some of the time spent at the home computer or in front of the television for a nice refreshing walk around the neighborhood. Make that time pleasurable—pet a dog, wave hello to a neighbor, or take some time to daydream about that tropical vacation you'd like to go on one day. The time you spend exercising will pass by before you know it!

Single parents arguably have less disposable time in their schedule. However, it can be possible to take the kids along on a walk. Make it fun for them, too: go to a nearby park, remind them they get time away from homework, or just play a fun, silly game of I Spy. Modeling good behavior and structuring healthy habits into your kids' routine can help set them up for better choices down the road, too.

From the standpoint of a company, systems that encourage employee health will not only help with your insurance premiums but will also lead to an increase in productivity. Exercise provides a natural boost in mood and energy because of its restorative capabilities within the brain. Eating healthier will similarly increase overall health, thereby improving mood and functionality.

Some companies partner with local health clubs and either subsidize employee membership or work a deal with the club to offer a volume discount on membership dues. Your insurance carrier may have tracking apps and programs to reward employee healthy habits with premium discounts. A company's bonuses or performance awards may be based on physically healthy habits.

Even something as simple as offering healthy snacks in the break room can teach employees to make better choices. Rarely will the everyday person choose an apple over a candy bar, but nuts, dried fruit, and granola make tasty alternatives that are filling and not as energy depleting as doughnuts or chocolates. Yes, healthy food is costly for the company, but only in the short run; in the long run, encouraging healthy food choices will benefit the company.

As mentioned before, one of the three maxims mentioned at the Temple of Apollo is "Nothing in excess." These days, we shorten it to one simple word: moderation.

Your body and your brain are the vehicles that are going to carry you through the journey we all share on this planet. If those parts aren't healthy, or performing at their ultimate, it will keep you from reaching your goal.

I believe the mind is different from the brain. You can remove the skull cap on a cadaver and see the brain inside. In adults, it weighs about three pounds, and all will grow with nearly the same structures. In the physical sense, we all have that in common. But the mind goes well beyond the physical structure of the brain itself. It is the totality of our experiences as a unique person. It is our memories, our emotions, our thoughts, and our ambitions.

Keep your mind healthy with the quality of the thoughts you pass through it. Keep your thoughts positive and turned toward the well-being of others. Your thoughts are food for your mind. If you pollute your mind with a constant stream of junk food (negativity, resentment, pessimism), then your mind's health will suffer. If you feed it good, healthy foods (positivity, empathy, optimism), then it will be strong and flourish.

For the mind to function, the physical brain itself needs to work at its full potential. This brings us back to taking care of your physical health.

People ask me all the time about how I can maintain such a high level of energy. In 2021, I celebrated my 70th birthday. My body is fit, and I am still able to do many of the physical things I was able to do when I was in my forties because I did my best to take care of myself. I didn't use a magical formula–I have worked hard to keep my body healthy.

Back in 1979, I stopped eating beef, pork, and veal. Michael Bolton recommended I try going without any red meat. He's a total vegan, but I still eat poultry and fish. I would tell the wait staff at restaurants, "If it flies or swims, I can eat it."

That's about the only restriction I have for my physical health. I've been blessed with a fast metabolism and the ability to know when I have had enough. I don't go on any diets; I eat until I am full, stop, and don't overeat. I also take my time when I'm eating. Word to the wise: eat in moderation. Enjoy the bounty of life!

***

Aside from diet, exercise, and sleep, help yourself and your employees deal with relieving immediate stress. Stress is one of the most often-cited reasons for poor eating habits. Alcohol and carbohydrate-heavy foods can have a short-term calming effect, but they also have the long-term negative side effects of weight gain, increased hunger response, and lowered energy. What is a healthier alternative to coping and releasing stress? The obvious answer again is still diet, exercise, and sleep.

For a short-term solution, we turn to the world of physiology and psychology.

This is where the sympathetic and the parasympathetic nervous systems come into play. To be clear, the word sympathetic used here is not the emotional response to someone's feelings you understand.

In this context, this is the part of our autonomic nervous system. The autonomic nervous system takes care of all the involuntary things our body does, like making the heartbeat, breathing, and dilating the pupils in our eyes. The autonomic nervous system is made up of two parts: the sympathetic and the parasympathetic. The sympathetic system gives our body the juice it needs, mainly epinephrine and norepinephrine, to act quickly to a threat. When the threat is gone, the parasympathetic system is what helps us relax and bring us back to a normal state. This is a very, very simplified explanation of how our fight-or-flight response works.

The fight-or-flight response was an enormously useful feature when we were getting chased around by wooly mammoths and sabre-toothed cats. The problem in the 21st century is that the fight-or-flight response can be triggered by common, everyday stress. So even if we maintain a sedentary lifestyle and experience very few opportunities to get eaten by a bear, our body still reacts to any perceived danger.

Modern-day stress continually bombards our autonomic nervous system with a lot of epinephrine, norepinephrine, cortisol, adrenaline, and many other chemicals. Over time, this puts our body through a lot of strain and breaks it down. We aren't built to be running at top speed all the time. The human body is like a car engine. It lasts longer if you set the cruise control at a steady speed, instead of gunning the engine and then letting it off constantly and continually.

For those of us living under the stress monster, engaging the parasympathetic nervous system can help bring the body back to a state of calm, thus putting it in a much healthier place.

Again, a good mindset is the best long-term solution. Re-examining how you interpret events and putting a positive spin on them—with the resulting belief in a positive outcome—will keep you from feeling the constant stress in the first place.

If you do find yourself tense, give these two things a try.

First, take three deep breaths. Draw the breath in through your nose, wait a couple beats, then let it out slowly through the mouth. If this sounds like some hokum you've heard a hundred times before, consider this: How do you feel after a good, deep yawn? You feel good, don't you? A deep yawn helps you feel relaxed, and probably a little high. Yawning triggers the same parasympathetic, "calm down" mechanisms in our brain. A deep cleansing breath will do the same thing.

Second, put yourself completely within the moment, in the here and now. Too often, stress can creep up while looking into the future and anticipating a negative event or outcome. Other times, when ruminating over the regret of the past, stress can drown you. So, rather than live in the future or wallow through the past, grab this moment right in front of you and live in the present. Focus on the physical sensations of your body sitting in your chair. Feel the chair against your back. Feel your rear end pushing down on the seat. Feel your feet against the floor. If your shirt is a little tight around your shoulders, feel those sensations, too. Focus on all these sensations to bring your mind into the present.

This exercise only takes about 90 seconds out of your day. If you don't have time to do a full yoga routine followed by a hot bath, this simple, brief action can bring an island of calm into the middle of your day without much time or energy required.

***

Your psyche is now a garden of infinite peace and tranquility, thanks to deep breathing exercises and bringing yourself into the here-and-now. One last cleansing breath, and all is well within you.

Then you open your eyes.

You've managed to quell the inner stress, but the outer stress is a tangled mass of chaos that looks like the back of an over-wired, ten-year-old, IT nightmare of a network server had a baby with the uncleaned, uncleared refrigerator in the breakroom filled with a variety of science experiments that were once someone's lunch.

Time to clear your business' stress mess with good organizational skills and smart planning. But how do you accomplish that? How do you know you are achieving the company's goals? You do so by using the process of operationalizing the procedure. Operationalize is a research design term that simply means the people involved in a particular project must specify the concrete methods used to measure and achieve the goal that the company has set.

Dave Wolff presented this lesson of discovery by how he managed Cyndi Lauper. He was deliberate and tactical with the way he promoted her. He never—and I mean never—wavered in his belief that she was going to be a notable platinum selling artist and top touring musical act in the world. Thus, he developed a specific game plan based on his belief, then executed it the best way he could.

156

His first and most important lesson: be specific with goals. Specificity is necessary to accomplish the goal in a gradual and deliberate manner. Your overall goal can be to make enough money to get through the next fiscal period. Your goal can be to invest in positive and constructive solutions for the community. Your goal can be to create a product that is useful to all people, no matter who or where they may be. Your first step in operationalizing is defining the goal.

Next, create a concrete action plan. Every business plan requires you to think through and write out the process you will put in place to achieve these goals. You need not only the steps to achieve success, but the steps you will take to ensure the steps leading to success are available. If you need specialized machinery to produce your product, how will you raise the capital and then secure the machine? Or how will it get shipped to your facility? Will the new machine need to be installed or assembled properly? Will you need specialized insurance to cover the workers operating the machine? Will your product require a patent once the machine begins cranking them out? Will you even have a facility for the machine before it arrives?

Next, communicate with those involved in the action plan. Ask what they need to get started. Once they get going, don't leave them to sink or swim–keep the communication line open. Is the plan working? Should any processes be changed?

Finally, once the goal is reached, it's time to resolve. Again, communicate with the employees on the team. Listen attentively to how they speak about the results of the plan. Was the goal ultimately reached? How did they feel about the process itself? Are they using positive words that look optimistically toward the company's future, or are they evasive or dire with their outlook?

How will you know if operationalizing worked? How do you accurately assess the progress? These goals are all easily measurable. The answers to these questions can be quantified with the help of your analytics team. Have them gather sales or usage figures as their data and run the numbers through a statistics generator. The results can demonstrate whether or not your customers are enjoying the fruit of your labor and engaging with your product

Chapter 13: Service and Altruism

Every good turn in my life has been the result of me treating someone like a human being. Service is the act of practicing altruism—selfless acts of kindness for others without an expectation of anything in return.

In a business, the overall goal is to raise the productivity of the entire staff, from the newest intern to the most seasoned board member. But, to truly raise productivity, remember this ancient saying: "A rising tide lifts all ships." If the overall morale of the company is positive, everyone is in a better mood, which infuses more energy into the task at hand. If morale is poor, employees will isolate themselves (sometimes into cliques), go at a snail's pace with less efficiency, and bring down the value of your product or service. Managers may find that they burn their own energy trying to manage the negativity as they attempt to do their primary job. Bosses who are controlling and only invested in self-interest create this atmosphere.

Duplicity and insincerity are not limited to the corporate environment. Do you have a friend or relative who only calls you when they need something? Or only asks about you as a springboard to telling you about them. They ignore your response because now they have a portal to talk about their agenda. You may know someone who will do you a favor but leave you with the sneaking suspicion that you now owe them one. Employees can sniff out a disingenuous boss just as they can sniff out disingenuous friends or relatives.

Conversely, employees can spot a genuine leader. They can tell if someone is interested in them or their perspective at work. Simple acts of kindness, like asking about them and remembering a detail about them can be huge. As the world speeds up, these kinds of genuine relationships become scarce. Remember that it takes time to build trust in a relationship. Trust will develop for trustworthy people. Be that patient person.

Treating others with dignity and respect may not come back to you in an immediate and tangible way—it is a long-term return on investment. Your commitment to the employee becomes recognition as a good and effective leader. Your peers will see you as reliable. This attribute can separate you from the rest. Someday, someone you barely remember may return to your life and return the altruism.

Dave in the Doorway is a story that fits this concept perfectly. He wasn't Paul McCartney standing and waiting to talk to me. He was a guy I'd never met before; a fan with a camera and an autograph book. He had a simple request, and I honored that request. I wasn't about to dismiss or ignore Dave. Everyone deserves respect. Yet, people often get dismissed. This unfortunate societal trend can open an amazing opportunity for you. People remember moments of dignity because it leaves an impression.

I left such an impression on Dave in the Doorway. Had I paid attention to him for personal gain, he'd walk away thinking I was smarmy. But I took time out of my schedule for him. I lifted his spirit by treating him with respect. He never forgot—and when he had a chance to be kind to me, he jumped at it.

***

Carrying a mindset geared toward serving others will always create a return of positivity to your life. It may not be on your timetable, and it may not be directly proportional to your act of kindness, but opportunities will come to you. You will have the chance to reap the harvest of your kindness and service.

It is simple to be kind to people and put their needs ahead of yours. It doesn't have to take a lot of time, it doesn't have to incur a big cost, and it doesn't have to involve a huge calorie burn. Moments of altruistic behavior cost nearly nothing but can be of infinite value to the recipient.

I repeat: Your kindness can be of infinite value to the recipient.

Imagine if everyone engaged in these acts toward each other. Imagine the cumulative effect of that emotional currency being passed back and forth.

It can change a life.

What can seem like insignificant moments, encounters, gestures, comments, and emails could transform your life for the better. One of those moments could also alter another person's life for the better. What seems like a fleeting, nonsensical moment to you may be a momentous event that brings the other person off a ledge.

We cannot always know what is happening in someone else's life. That is why we must learn to be free in giving kindness and empathy. That small piece of goodness may be all that a fellow human being needs to keep themselves together.

Reflect on a significant moment in your life that you feel you could never forget. Maybe it was a moment you shared with one of your parents or siblings. Maybe it was a conversation you had with a friend or a lesson you teacher gave.

The reason you remember this occasion is because of its impact on your life. You lived it, and you remembered it again later. You may have told a friend or family member about the moment. You revisited the moment several times since it occurred. The remembrance is an artifact of the importance.

Realize the importance of this singular moment, especially compared to the immeasurable number of events and moments in your life that you have zero recollection of. Most moments of our lives flow past like water under a bridge. However, some particular moments will stand out.

Focus on a moment that involved one of your parents (or any caregiver you've had in your life). Whether it was good or bad, it was still a memory that held significance in your life. Psychologists have a name for this: the autobiographical memory.

Many autobiographical memories are subtle–a takeaway that was profound in its simplicity. Do you think your parents or caregiver would remember the moment, too? They may not. To them, that was just another sentence in a brief conversation with you in the front yard. Or maybe a joke shared at the dinner table. That person had a thousand other things going on in their life, so this moment was neither here nor there for them. They wouldn't cruelly dismiss your memory; they just simply didn't hold onto it. But to you, it was a time you'll never forget.

Because of incidents like that, I strongly remind people that you cannot predict what small actions or words will be impactful for the people around you. Your children pay attention even when you think they're watching television or a computer. Your employees are watching and listening even when you think they're reading an email or typing up the cover to their TPS report. When you address your employees, your words are taken seriously. You are not "one of them." You're the leader.

At home, you're not your child's buddy. You're their parent.

Psychologists also have a term for this: the power dynamic. It describes how someone in an authoritative position affects the interactions within a relationship between two or more people using influence and control. These interactions can be positive as well as negative.

161

Take your role as a person in charge seriously and be careful to put your best foot forward. This role is not just a mask you wear when you're at work or at home. Being in charge can easily put even the kindest of souls into a harmful mindset. Find it within yourself to make this power an article of faith that silently guides all your decisions and interactions.

Why, of course I have a cool story about that exact thing!

***

While I was on Cyndi Lauper's Fun Tour, in support of the She's So Unusual album, we played a gig at The Meadowlands in New Jersey. Whenever I played around New York or New Jersey, I would invite my family to come out and watch the show. At that time, Cyndi's tour was obviously the biggest event I had ever been a part of. When she came to town, my family was eager to see me on the big stage with an established superstar.

My mother's attendance was a big deal to me. She had sacrificed so much to get me to this point. It still brings tears to my eyes to think about all she did for me.

Cyndi was on fire that night, being the best version of herself. After the show, I brought Mom backstage and introduced her to Cyndi. She is half Italian, so she embraced my mother and immediately fell into a comfortable—albeit energetic—conversation about recipes. It still cracks me up to recount the chatter.

Mom: "Your mother is Italian, Cyndi?"

Cyndi: "Yup! She sure is!"

Mom: "Does she know how to make gravy?"

Cyndi: "Well…we call it sauce."

Mom: "Oh, no, no, no!"

Their conversation was so warm and authentic, like two women from the old country getting together over a nice cup of coffee and a cannoli.

They came to a pause in the conversation, and my mom asked if Cyndi would mind signing a picture for her. Cyndi, being who she is, agreed without hesitation.

I had brought a picture for Cyndi to sign just in case the need arose. It was a simple 8x10 black-and-white glossy photo of Cyndi and me. The picture was taken during a television appearance, and it shows

162

The actual photo Cyndi signed for my mother

Close-up of Cyndi's message to Mom

me playing drums and Cyndi sitting in front of the drum kit on a riser. We are both laughing in the photo–a wonderful moment that captured our personalities in a single frame.

Cyndi grabbed it and scribbled her signature, along a quick personal note to my mom. The inscription read: *To Sadie—Your son is great. XOXO, Cyndi!*

The whole signature took Cyndi maybe twelve seconds. To her, it was neither here nor there. It was a kind gesture she would have done for any fan. Celebrity status didn't spoil her.

I slid the photo into an envelope and turned it over to Mom, who accepted it like Moses taking the stone tablets from the hand of God.

Mom called me the minute she got home from the venue. She was almost without words.

"I…I can't believe…Sandy, Cyndi really likes you!"

I couldn't help but smile on my end of the phone. "Oh yeah, Ma? What did she write?"

"Well…your…your son is great."

My smile widened. "Yeah? That's awesome, Ma!"

For my mom, a woman who lost her husband early on and raised her children by herself as she worked her fingers to the bone doing labor-intensive jobs, this was a defining moment for her.

Me and Mom

When I was a kid, Mom never complained when I was in the basement loudly pounding away at my drums. She would just flick the lights on and off when it was time to come up for supper. Come to think of it, my mother never complained about anything. She was not a bitter or resentful person. She did what was needed to be done for her children out of pure love.

Cyndi's experience was barely a ripple in the pond of her life. But for my mother, it was a monumental tsunami. Receiving that picture from Cyndi Lauper was the culmination of Mom's life's work with me. It validated everything she had done, and it was proof that her son was successful and happy.

If pride had physical substance, she would have burst from it.

My mother used to carry that picture around with her everywhere. She got a cardboard insert so the photo wouldn't get bent or damaged. It came with her to church meetings and when she went to play Canasta or Po-ke-no with her friends. She would gather the other ladies around and pull the picture out of the envelope. Then she would talk about it with the same reverence as if she was putting the Hope Diamond around her own neck.

"Look! Look what Cyndi Lauper thinks of my son!"

When my mother died, she had that picture in a frame in her bedroom. I took it with me as a memento of my life with Mom. It still hangs in my office at home.

Those few precious seconds it took Cyndi to interact and sign that picture for my mother had a lasting impression. To Cyndi, it was no big deal. To my mother, it held an incalculable value.

My mother raised two daughters and a son. She did everything for us. She mentored, scolded, fed, loved, and protected us every day of our lives together.

And now, look what Cyndi Lauper thinks of her son!

I can only hope I'm able to lift the spirit of somebody the way Cyndi lifted my mom. I don't know if Cyndi even realizes the effect she had. I hope to tell her someday. Knowing Cyndi like I do, she will be honored to have played that role.

The lesson here is that Leaders have this same power—the power to uplift. Take a moment to encourage. It goes a long way!

***

A universal principle that all human beings should subscribe to is Take Responsibility. If you are given a certain job to do—whether you're in a band, in an office, or in a family—you take ownership of the task and make sure it's completed. If the job is outside of your ability, for whatever reason, ask for help. Asking for help is far easier than formulating excuses for poorly executed work.

The sphere of responsibility encompasses not just the responsible individual, it holds an entire community. We are all in the community together, whether we are in a band, work in an office, attend school, or have a family. Because we are all members of the community, we all share responsibility for its success.

If you see a task that needs to be done, but it lies outside of the exact parameters of your "job," then redefine your parameters, get up, and get the job done. Be tenacious. Help each other out. Take the ball and run with it.

Excuses that drive me crazy:

"Well…that's not my job."

"Nope…that has nothing to do with me."

"So-and-so should have done it."

"Well...so-and-so never did anything for me."

"I didn't feel like doing it."

Hopefully, because you are a hard-working person committed to a solid work ethic, you read this list of excuses and think, do people really say such things? Do they really believe this is a reasonable answer to anything? Yes. This happens, and it happens more often than you'd think. This avoidance occurs on all levels of corporate structure, from the executive boardroom to the intern's break room. It is done out of entitlement, convenience, disinterest, or (in some extreme cases) trauma, fear of failure, and shame. And it is never productive.

Be strong; own your accountability! You are not selfish or self-centered—if you were, you would not be interested in this book! You lead by example. Whether the task is big or small, it has to be done—and that's the point. You must either take care of it yourself or alert someone if you can't do it yourself.

The motivation behind responsibility is not for the acclaim. Those who constantly remind the manager of every little thing they do for the company garner no respect from their co-workers or their manager. Taking responsibility because you are "owed a favor" is a poor motivation, as well. Collecting this kind of debt is not a healthy way to go through life, and it will make people reluctant to lend you a hand. If they know you will lord the favor over them until the debt is repaid, they will steer clear of you for any reason, much less asking a favor.

Beware of letting yourself to slip into a "not my issue" mindset. Warning signs are a lack of interest, denying mistakes, avoiding a challenge, wallowing in self-pity, and complaining of unfairness. Do what you have to do to regain your confidence. Be the one who steps up to the plate!

I had the experience of stepping in and doing what I thought was a little thing. At the time, the task seemed small, and it didn't take long to do, nor did it take any effort. But it turned out to be quite important.

One of a stage manager's many responsibilities is to set out water and towels for the stage performers. About ten minutes before show time, he makes sure everyone has a bottle of water and a clean towel at their station. It's not a complex job, but it's very important for those of us sweating under the hot lights.

Added to this simple task is the crazy issue of water preference. Some performers liked their water cold, and some liked it room temperature. Cyndi liked her water to be placed on the edge of the

166

drum riser. Other singers like the water to be at the foot of their mic stand. One guitar player I worked with liked his water to be on his amp.

The stage manager keeps track of all those water preferences as part of his duty list. Performing artists tend to want things exactly the same night in and night out. That way, they don't have to burn any mental or emotional calories trying to find their water. If everything remains consistent from show to show, then the performers can focus on giving a great performance.

Consistency can be an important factor in everyone's work and home life. The more random the workload gets, or the more chaotic events at home become, the more stress it all creates. This quickly wears down your health, both mental and physical.

When I was on the road with Joan Jett, we played a show one night where everything was off. Random things went wrong, and Jimmy the stage manager ran around like a chicken with its head cut off. The poor guy was pulled in a hundred different directions all at once.

First issue: Joan's monitor went out. There's no telling how it went haywire between the sound check and the stage appearance, but it was critical to the show and to Joan. It was up to Jimmy to fix the problem. Stressed out and muttering to himself, he jogged past me.

It wasn't like Jimmy to be so frazzled. So, I asked him what was up.

"Ah, Joan's fucking monitor went out."

"Oh, wow! Sorry, man."

"Yeah," he sighed. Just as he started to run again, he said to me, "...and I still got to get the fucking water on the stage in ten minutes!"

I yelled back to him. "I'll take care of it!"

He stopped short and turned, his brow furrowed, and his eyes squinted. "No, Sandy, you don't have to go out there in front of the audience!"

"I'll take care of it," I insisted.

With a huge look of relief, he nodded once and headed for the accursed monitor.

I did it, just as I said I would. I grabbed the water bottles and towels and strolled out on stage like I was just minding my own business.

The crowd, upon seeing me, started to cheer. I gave a goofy little bow, then waved to the excited multitude. I then signaled to them that

I was just tidying up and doing some housekeeping items ahead of the performance. No need to get excited just yet.

The crowd was fine with that, so they patiently waited for the show to start. When it did, the monitor was fixed, we all had water and towels, and we gave the crowd our usual best!

Earlier, when I saw Jimmy run past me, he was so exasperated. He had the weight of the world on his shoulders, and probably no idea how he was going to take care of the monitor and the water and the towels. I could've easily shrugged my shoulders and told the flustered stage manager, "Oh, Jimmy! Dude, that's fucked up. You better hurry."

Honestly, it was all I was obligated to say. We could have had a three-second exchange, and then I would have gone back to thinking about the set list or preparing myself for the performance. Those were the technical limits of my job. The end of my responsibility.

Jimmy himself didn't expect me to help. Frankly, he didn't need my help. But my friend and stage manager was behind the eight ball, and I saw the opportunity to relieve him of some pressure. We took care of business, and the band moved smoothly into another great performance.

Also, I just can't turn my back on a friend and co-worker who is in a tough spot. I wasn't raised that way. This was my mindset. If everything I do is guided by the knowledge that I will take responsibility for the success of the band, then the other band members will notice and join in.

In your own life, you know the people you can count on and the people who always look for an angle. You notice. You especially notice their intent. A responsible-acting person may try to be humble. A person with an angle may try to appear genuine. But they can't camouflage their intentions. At least, they can't do it long term. It'll eventually show.

I knew Jimmy appreciated my help. I could tell by the look on his face. It was enough for me, and it made me feel good. We each have a little match burning in our soul. When two people hold their flames together, the fire burns hotter and brighter.

I realize that I'll get push-back on this concept. People have been burned by helping others. Helping others altruistically shows you're a pushover, a schlemiel, and a glutton for punishment. Here's where I push back. There's a big difference between being taken advantage of and acting altruistically without sacrificing your own well-being.

168

No one should say "yes" to everything. No one deserves to get walked on over and over and say "thank you" each time. True strength comes from having firm but flexible boundaries with people, empathy for mistakes, and an ability to cauterize your own wounds.

I implore everyone to stand up for what they believe in. Your ideas, your thoughts, and your beliefs can never be taken away from you–only you have the power to change your beliefs if you choose to do so. Hold your ground with your thoughts, and do not waver. Conviction is a part of your personal strength and well-being.

However, if you happen to get screwed over, your first reaction is going to be anger.

Speaking out against unfair treatment does feel good in the short term. It's okay to allow yourself a space and a moment to vent. It can be beneficial to release some steam immediately after something bad happens to you. Do it swiftly, then stop. From there, follow a path of serenity. Change the things you can change and accept the things you can't. Continuing to rant long-term will pull you down like quicksand. If you allow yourself to hop online and start writing social media posts about how so-and-so screwed you out of X number of dollars, you'll garner feedback from people who are similarly angry and want revenge against the people who wronged them. An echo chamber of vitriol is created, and you are worse off than if you just let it go and move on.

Some situations may not allow you to simply move on. You may want or need to seek resolution. Be smart and keep a cool head. Diplomacy is critical to keep you out of trouble. Let the other person decide whether or not they are interested in resolving the issue. Depending on their answer, you may find you'll need to seek legal advice and action. Be your own best advocate. Say what needs to be said in a forthright and non-aggressive way. This is where silence rarely accomplishes resolution. As my father used to say, "The squeaky wheel gets the most grease." Always remember, nobody cares about your situation more than you do, so make sure to tend to your own backyard. Keep your expectations realistic and be prepared to accept whatever outcome happens as a result.

After all your resources for resolution are exhausted, hold your head up, learn from the situation, and move forward. You are not a victim. You become a person with a strong internal set of standards and a moral compass. And you are always the better person.

On a personal note, I admit that I have dealt with managers who royally screwed me over and still to this day owe me money. After trying to get what was owed to me—and believe me, I tried every route available—I came to a crossroad. I could either spend more time and energy gnashing my teeth to whoever listened to my frustration. Or I could make my peace with the outcome and move on. Treading water in a pool of resentment and negativity would ultimately be what hurt me, not the offending managers.

The reputation of people like those managers also builds over time. I would never go out of my way to besmirch any of them. I don't have to. The way they do business speaks loud enough from all the folks they have screwed over. When I speak about that universal force, and how important it is to put good energy and positivity into the world, the opposite also holds true. Negative begets negative.

I firmly believe that, and it helps me move on.

I challenge you to take this to heart: When you do things altruistically, out of concern for other people, with no expectation of a return, then you actually appear stronger than a person who shirks responsibility and makes excuses.

***

Keep in mind that the reason anyone goes into business is to make money, whether it's a service, as with a doctor or nurse, or a product, such as a sandwich shop. Businesses are set up to make the lives of our customers better. The task of generating a profit is accomplished much more easily when our business adds value to people's lives.

Patients and their children are healthier because we are good doctors. Hungry lunch patrons go back to the office with happy, full bellies after eating our sandwiches. They exchange money for good service, or a solid product sold at a fair price. If both of those pieces are in order, the customers will come back. Repeat business is the lifeblood that keeps businesses alive.

These customers patronize one particular place instead of a competitor down the street because it betters their lives. On rare occasion, a unique or stellar product can overcome a poor customer experience, but only to a certain extent. Beyond that, most people will not put up with a surly cashier or front office worker, no matter how good the sandwich or the medical service is.

I firmly believe the inverse is also true. People will put up with food that might be just average, compared than the shop down the street, as long as they feel welcomed and comfortable in that shop. Have you ever been to a restaurant where the chef comes out and chats with the customers? If you're a regular, does the chef remember your name? Or perhaps she remembers a minor detail about you? Think about the impact of that 45-second conversation with the chef. Your sense of being welcomed and a part of the "team" is an invaluable marketing asset for the restaurant—it guarantees you'll be back.

Apply that concept, not only to your customers, but also to your employees. If you, as the manager, supervisor, or executive, have a 45-second positive interaction with your employee, the deeper impact can be priceless. Ask about them, their day, or their family. Do they have a kid in t-ball? Didn't they recently adopt a rescue puppy or kitty? The devil is in the details; don't underestimate the power of a relationship. It's both the cake with the icing—you and the employees working together. It's the why behind the what.

How do your customers feel when they encounter the first line employees? Do you hire and train people who make the lives of others better? What kind of first impression does your business impart on your customers?

You might have the best sandwiches in town, but a dirty shop with a low health department rating or a cranky staff member who aggravate customers will drive business away faster than bad food.

***

How do we create a spirit of altruism in our company?

Joan Jett used to take time to encourage and reinforce acts of kindness. I remember her grabbing me after one show to tell me how much she appreciated what I had done for a fan. She saw me go to my drum tech to ask for a drumstick. I went back out on stage and gave it to a fan. Not a big deal to me, but it was to Joan. This was exactly the kind of altruism she expected from her band and crew.

Why did Joan Jett care if I went out of my way to make a fan happy? Why did she step back and observe what I was doing, and then take a minute to congratulate me on an act of kindness? Because she knew that the better her people represented her and her brand, the better it reflected on her public appeal, which lead to an increased value in her brand.

As her drummer, I am an extension of Joan and her brand. If I blow off a fan, they don't really think about who Sandy Gennaro is. They tell their friends that the guy who plays drums in Joan Jett's band was a jerk. More than likely, the fan may not know my name. But it's Joan's name that becomes associated with the negative reaction.

I didn't create a huge financial windfall from giving a stick to a fan, but that wasn't my goal. I just wanted to make the fan feel happy and appreciated. Similar to what I've previously mentioned, goodwill begets goodwill.

Think about rock stars that have poor reputations. I don't need to dig through social media allegations. I know enough people on the "inside" who know exactly which musicians are easy and which ones are are difficult to deal with.

Why does that matter? Good question. On the surface, reputation seems to have little impact. Plenty of rock stars draw negative press and scathing comments from critics still sell millions of albums and fill arenas. Athletes who have terrible interpersonal skills in the locker room and out in public still land high-paying contracts because of their ability in their chosen sport. Hundreds (or more) of musicians, athletes, and other celebrity professionals may be appropriately talented, but they're still public relations disasters. Eventually, these enfants terribles either wash out quickly or struggle to find a team, band, or label who will hire them.

The general public's opinion of your company is extremely important. After all, those people are the ones who pay for your goods or services. No one truly wants the hassle associated with a toxic personality.

If you're a good hang, no doubt you are a person who practices kindness and altruism. You have developed the habit of self-awareness. You understand the point of view of the people around you, and act accordingly to nurture a positive perspective.

When Joan gave me words of affirmation for giving away the drumstick, she was letting me know that additional behavior toward that end would benefit her, and ultimately, me! After all, she was the owner and CEO of the company that kept me employed.

***

Recognition is a potent form of motivation. If a Boss makes an employee feel expendable, they'll work like an employee that is expendable. If a Boss doesn't think they're special, why should they even try to be special? It won't make a difference for either the employee or the Boss.

Yet, if an employee feels valued and validated, they will work accordingly.

Give sincere praise to positive performances. Fuel the fire each of us has in our soul. A positive slant instead of a negative focus makes everyone around you better.

That seemingly small act of verbal service costs you nothing but creates value and benefit for those who receive it.

A quick act of kindness can take roughly three to five minutes, but the return on the investment is immeasurable. Like any investment, there is a small risk—you can't predict the outcome. The best way to ensure that your kindness investment is not for self-gain is to give when your heart is so full, you can't hold it all. Give because you believe that abundance is worth sharing. Give because, deep down, you really want the other person's life to be better. And have faith that your gift will return to you.

***

At the end of each stage show I've performed in, the band walks to the front of the stage and takes a bow to show the audience our gratitude. I might shake hands or slap a few hi-fives and then toss a couple drum sticks into the crowd, too.

In my mind, this is a nominal act; it's no big deal. With a simple flick of my wrist, I send the sticks out into the crowd of fans to share the love. I am careful to toss them gently (not a good idea to hurl them like wooden javelins), but I'll give a couple of underhand tosses and call it a night.

Following one show, I walked to the front of the stage and noticed a woman in a wheelchair. She wore a big smile, and was clapping her hands, nearly bouncing out of her chair with excitement. There was a purity in her smile, and I felt moved in that moment. We made eye contact and I tossed a drum stick directly to her.

Later, I received word from her husband, Mike Pierce. He found me on Facebook and sent a message recounting how important that interaction brought his handicapped wife such joy. That little drumstick toss was a beaming highlight for her. She was having a shadowbox made for it, and she couldn't wait to hang it up to show their friends.

Later, Mike and I got together when he happened to travel through Nashville. We had the most engaging conversation, highlighted by his

173

work in the public speaking industry. I had dabbled in it, and I had a strong interest in learning more about public speaking. Mike had a good grip on my attention. I recounted my Dave in the Doorway story and how it led to working with Cyndi Lauper. Not once did Mike look away from me or change the subject—he was sold. He found the story to be powerful and urged me to pursue a speaking career. And he gladly offered his help.

I launched a speaking career because of my relationship with Mike. To this day, I consider him a friend and mentor. His help in getting me organized and on the road to the speaker circuit cannot be measured. But it originated from a single opportunity where I tossed a drum stick to a fan in a wheelchair.

I never underestimate the fan experience. I see how important that tossed drumstick can be. I am gracious, upbeat, and positive when I interact with the fans. That may be their only interaction with me. Heck, it could be their only interaction with someone they think is a celebrity. So, I make it count. I do so in honor of the moments Cyndi shared with my mother.

***

I have demonstrated how important Carmine Appice was to me. And I did my best to repay him in kind. I doubt I could ever balance the scales; I owe him for getting my professional career started. Still, I don't forget the kind gesture gifted to me, and I do what I can to return in kind.

Thanks to Carmine's reference, I secured a gig with Blackjack. Before I left for New York to audition, Carmine gave me a call. He asked how I was doing because he heard about my nightmare audition with Rod Stewart. I was still depressed. Even though I was about to audition, Blackjack had yet to exist. I was so low, my feet dangled off the curb.

No matter how dejected I get, I never forget that my friends need support, too.

"You know, Carmine, I don't think Rod's band has found a drummer yet. You should go for that gig. I think you'd be great."

I didn't have the phone number for Rod's management, but I had the number of Gary Grainger, Rod's guitar player. Carmine called Gary, who confirmed that, yes, they still needed a drummer. Carmine went down to the studio, auditioned, and got the gig. Not only did he perform for the tour of Rod's album, A Night on the Town, but he ended up playing on Rod's next four studio albums, as well. All those albums combined sold eight million copies. Carmine also earned a writing credit on the mammoth number one hit, "Do Ya Think I'm Sexy." The single itself sold over three million copies.

When we help those we care about, we ultimately help ourselves. This selfless act is altruism. People supporting each other without a hidden agenda of expecting a reward in return.

I didn't foresee Carmine's name on my resume resulting in an audition for the Blackjack gig. I'm not clairvoyant. I only wanted to help him out as much as I could because he was (and still is) my friend.

A touch of kindness was all it took to nudge one domino into the next, leading to a fortuitous chain reaction. Carmine helped me fall into the Blackjack gig. While recording with Blackjack, I fell into Benny Mardones.

And the BEATS of the falling dominos continue.

PART III: THE PIVOT
Chapter 14: Adapting to Change

Several times I've been asked to develop a one- or two-hour talk on adapting to change. Between developing technology, working from home, and the ubiquitous shifts to our society caused by the COVID-19 pandemic, many have struggled with new and different ways of working and living. To survive, we had to adapt to change.

Few people are as familiar with adapting to change as a touring musician—especially contract musicians who receive a 1099 form at the end of the tax year.

Anyone who has made their living on the road understands the pivots required to survive any unforeseen obstacles thrown in your path. Delayed flights, missed connections, inclement weather, and inexplicable technology wreak havoc on a traveler who insists their world remain unspoiled by change. It doesn't matter if you're a musician, a motivational speaker, a java programmer, or the proprietor of a French bakery—the ability to flex when life applies pressure is critical.

You can never anticipate all the things that could go wrong. We're not psychics (and I have a hard time believing those really exist). Instead, you adjust your mindset regarding how you approach these different and unexpected situations. We must separate cognition from perception, or reason from emotion. We problem solve.

Problem solving has two distinct parts. First, it requires an honest appraisal of options with a careful weighing of pros and cons. Second, it requires action.

For example, you discover your flight is delayed. As with most flights these days, a tardy flight means you may miss a connection. You're under pressure to get from Cleveland to Nashville for an important event, meeting, or gig. In response to your anxiety, your heart speeds up.

In that moment, panic is certainly an option—frustration is inevitable. Take a second to breathe and center yourself before smashing your internal Oh, Crap! button. You are now ready to assess options and compare the pros and cons.

If your meeting is first thing the next morning, you could jump into a rental car and drive to Nashville. It could be dangerous; the drive may take eight to nine hours in the dark of night on roads you may not be familiar with. During that time, you really should be sleeping. If you manage to not fall asleep at the wheel, you'll get to the meeting. However, you'll be bleary-eyed, caffeine infused, and as laser focused as a fruit fly. But you will be at that meeting!

Or you can peruse other flights on the schedule. Nestled inside the pockets of nearly every modern traveler is a powerful computer. It opens a world of possibilities, especially when it comes to rebooking flights. Add to it the Frequent Fliers who have even more options due to the benefits granted to them by their airline because of their elite status At least, it can feel elite, like a backstage pass or having your name on the doorman's list at the club. Never least at all is the airport concierge who can make the problem go away for the harried, but kind-hearted, traveler.

Finally, one last option stands: don't go to the meeting. Bad for many people, sure, but this option isn't necessarily catastrophic. For me, as a musician, it is imperative that I get to the gig. Like anyone else, I've been sick, wiped out, or otherwise compromised, but I powered through and played the gig. Still, if I absolutely, positively cannot make a gig, the band's or artist's manager will find a drummer in that city who can learn the charts quickly and be there in my stead.

The loss looks bad on the surface but is manageable for a rational person.

This scenario is a deep dive into a common issue airline travelers face every day. If you are a seasoned road-and-air warrior, you're nodding to the familiarity of the options in the section. However, the meticulous presentation of these options walks you through the first process of problem solving—assess options and weigh the costs and benefits. Once you've gone through that, all that's left is to decide and act.

However, one option I left out because I really think using the option of acting like a spoiled toddler who needs a nap is the worst idea ever.

I've traipsed through many airports many times because of my career. I cannot stand the noise of a person loudly berating the poor ticket agent behind the counter because of a flight delay. The person who does this takes all their dignity and maturity, throws it into the garbage, and chooses the least effective solution anyone could choose—pitching a very public temper tantrum. Yes, traveling is tiring and stressful, but that's no excuse for bad behavior. I remember a pilot once telling me that, if he sees this happening, he'll don his uniform hat and stand beside the agent, especially if the delay is taking forever. The people in line tend to calm down. They assume The Man With The Hat Behind The Counter is an authority figure who will straighten out this awful inconvenience. It would be funny if it weren't for the ugly reality of how little respect is given to customer service employees, especially airline ticket agents.

Thank goodness, you and I know better. We adapt to change without wasting energy on blame. Inconvenience does not equal impossibility.

This is a very important concept to teach to your whole staff, from the topmost executives to the newest team members—and to your children, if you are a parent. It is a reminder of the tenacity needed to overcome adversity.

***

I am very grateful for the opportunity to have performed with so many talented artists. I am humbled by all my experiences, and I am proud of my music community. A cool trait that ties us together is the strong ability to adapt. Change is the greatest teacher; she provides the education everyone needs in their lives. Adaptability is requisite to make it as a rock and roll musician, and I'd like to show how it helps us.

The size of a music tour depends on factors like budget, locations, attendance, popularity of the artist, and so on. The Pat Travers Band's tour qualified as medium-sized. On a medium-sized tour, the budget doesn't allow individual band members to bring their own "back line" (drums and amps/sound system) equipment along. Those set-ups are big and heavy, and they require a truck to haul them from gig to gig, a local crew for set up and tear down, plus the requisite unpacking and packing, and overseas shipping if the band goes on a European tour. To avoid this overhead, the band has a few options. They can rent backline equipment from a local company. They can rent the equipment from the venue itself. They can borrow the backline equipment of another act on the bill. Often, the opening act is local. As the band's drummer, I would use the drum set the opening drummer brought with him. That way, the band just travels with guitars; all I travel with is drumsticks. I always have a rider in the contract that specifies exactly what I want regarding my drums, and exactly how I want them set up.

But, as we all know, things don't always go as planned.

Sometimes the opening act would have a high-quality drum set.

179

The drummer's dad may have purchased a top-shelf Neal Peart rig. Other times, the drum set I sat behind was a total disaster, but I'd make do as best I could.

Honestly, it doesn't matter what kind of drums I'd play. The important part is how they are set up. Every drummer likes their drum kit measured out and set up in a particular and unique way. The height of the snare, the positioning of the ride cymbal, the angle of the foot pedals, the toms, and so on. All of us have our set-up particulars.

I would always approach the opening-act drummer and ask, in a polite, non-confrontational way, if they'd mind playing their set using my configurations on their gear. It's a big and intrusive request, but I always did my best to considerately ask for what I wanted so that my needs would be met.

Some drummers would recognize me and be delighted to change their set up if I would sign their snare head or a couple sticks for them. Some had no idea who I was, but knew I was with the headliner, so that drummer would treat me as a guest and gladly help.

This worked nine times out of ten, but the occasional push-back would happen. Some drummers simply wanted no part in accommodating anyone who wanted to change their rig. I get it—that set belongs to them, and it's an investment in their career they needed to protect.

Drum set-up wasn't the only touring snag I dealt with. I had constant adjustments on my part: different venues, different local crews, different acoustics, travel nightmares, bad food, and trying to manage life back home. I never knew what would fly at me next.

Change is necessary to keep us fresh and alert. Monotony leads to distraction and complacency. For a touring musician, if there isn't at least some change happening, we get stale and bored, playing the same songs the same way night after night.

Another instance: Cyndi Lauper and Joan Jett are both enormously successful musicians, but each take a different approach to the way their stage show is played.

Cyndi wanted every song to be played the same way every night. The tunes had to precisely mirror the recorded albums. She would dance or move differently within the framework of the song, but she wanted to band to create a consistent framework.

Joan wanted the songs to be counted off with the correct tempo. She wanted the same start and end to the show every night. That was her framework. This gave the rest of the band the freedom to improvise and have some fun as long as we remained within the basic arrangement of the song.

How did this affect me? With Joan, I could create my own tweaks and changes every night to remain interested and in the moment. I embraced the small changes each night as I found different fills or cymbal accompaniments to make each performance unique.

With Cyndi, I wasn't allowed the space to change anything with the music during the song. I found other little ways to remain focused so my mind wouldn't wander. Sometimes I'd switch up from playing the snare with my left hand and high hat with my right to playing the snare with my right hand and the high hat with my left. This kept me engaged. This example may seem a little silly, but it worked.

Please understand that I am not ungrateful. Nothing could be further from the truth! I didn't think of Cyndi's idea of retaining consistency to be a negative. It was neither here nor there to me. I knew that's what she liked, so I adapted to her ideas. I looked forward to every night I walked onto that stage with her. She was fun to watch as she performed. Her focus was always on the fans. She was a consummate professional and the ultimate entertainer.

Change can be difficult, but the satisfaction it brings is worth it. We need a changing environment to keep our brains from wandering into a complacent, auto-pilot mode. It leads to progress and improvement. Can you imagine if no one had been willing to switch to painless dentistry or round wheels?

> *According to Darwin's Origin of Species, it is not the most intellectual of the species that survives; it is not the strongest that survives; but the species that survives is the one that is able best to adapt and adjust to the changing environment in which it finds itself.*
>
> *–Leon C. Megginson (1963)*

***

Stress is inherent in any growth model. The ability to manage the growth of a business becomes progressively more difficult for executives and business owners. Their managerial reach is spread thin across every aspect of the company's operations.

Despite her endless reserve of energy, Cyndi Lauper herself was not immune to this stress. I watched as she transformed from the micro-manager of a club band to a leader and delegator of a larger, in-demand band. After hitting so many bumps in the road, she adapted her mindset to personally overseeing every detail to delegating her authority. I remember Cyndi trying time after time to get the lighting crew to hit their cues on color changes. She was very specific on the color of light illuminating her on the stage at certain times during songs. She eventually learned to trust the people she and Dave put in place to take care of the small, peripheral matters.

Cyndi was accustomed to running the entire show by herself. When she was in Blue Angel, a bar and club band, she and her band mates were responsible for everything from bookings, to set up, to set list, to hiring a manager, to working out their eventual contract with Polydor Records. She felt the pressure to have every detail covered.

When she connected with Dave Wolff and recorded a multi-platinum record, she went from playing in front of hundreds of people to playing in front of 20,000 or more fans. She could no longer be responsible for every aspect of the show. It took time for her to stop feeling like she was responsible for every aspect of the show. It would drive her crazy when the mood lighting wasn't executed properly. I don't think the audience ever knew the difference, but to Cyndi, this kind of mistake was inexcusable.

She had to begin to let go. Delegation was not only stress-reducing, but necessary for her overall sanity. It was a difficult process; she was never too far away from being concerned about every facet of the performance. Yet over time, she learned which things she could let go of and which things she needed to stay on top of. Throughout the tour I spent with her, I watched her become more comfortable with adaptability.

***

The ability to adapt is rapidly becoming a key component to success. When COVID-19 hit, the entire world was forced to adapt and adjust. Some did it better than others, but no one had a choice in the matter. Those who made the pivot most effectively and smoothly seemed to gain an advantage over others who struggled with the transition.

In the world of corporate speaking and consulting, the generational gap within the workplace widened a great deal. Many companies have moved to a 100% digital platform. For the generations who grew up

182

immersed in computers and digital technology, this is not a problem. It is their mindset.

Some employees who belong to an older generation may be more comfortable with analog methods. For them, a pen and a pad of paper is their weapon of choice. As a result, companies have struggled to help the pen-and-paper crowd make the tough transition to a digital workplace. Companies that have executives and owners of this older mindset will struggle harder to stay in business. Fear of change is found at all levels.

Resistance to change can exact a toll on one's career. I have a cousin who is a doorman in Manhattan. Being a doorman is an excellent way to earn a living, especially if you enjoy engaging with people. Unfortunately, my cousin is not in that category. He left a six-figure Madison Avenue marketing job when his company switched to 100% digital software to create ad copy.

My cousin resisted the change. He still believes to this day that going to the literal drawing board was the only way to create marketing solutions for their high-power clients. However, the clients didn't want analog mockups anymore. They had grown to appreciate the quick changes, dynamic styles, and nearer-to-the-final look that digital platforms provided.

As you can imagine, this battle did not go well for my cousin. He is now a doorman. I still talk to him on the phone and listen to him complain about his lot in life.

I totally get where my cousin is coming from. In my industry, drum machines are not going away any time soon. For us drummers, we could either fight the system, or learn a little programming. By adapting and learning, we can be useful to producers who want some of the tracks digital and some tracks performed by a musician behind a real drum kit.

In fact, I wrote an article for Modern Drummer magazine (Gennaro, 1985) titled, "Approaching the Scary Monster." I addressed the necessity of change in any industry, and how we would do well to work with new technology rather than against it. I predicted that, despite being everyone's new popular toy, drum machines lacked a human feel. They would be incorporated into our profession rather than take it over. History proved my theory. By the end of the 1980s, the "electronic" sound lost its novelty, so a new hybrid approach was created to modern drumming. Human drummers were invited back to play alongside a track or use the track to maintain time.

Nowadays, almost every album incorporates some use of electronic drums as a time-keeping device. Producers still use programmed drums to create consistency and different sounds on albums. Not surprisingly, nearly every touring drummer in the industry also uses some kind of electronic timing system, or "click tracks," during live performances. None of us can argue the utility of the technology to keep a constant beat and to keep us honest and on track, so to speak.

Pun intended.

Adapt and survive. Or remain static and accept the consequences.

***

Many people may find change to be a challenge at first. It can take time for those people to accept change. I think the stages of adapting to change are very much like the stages of grief. This concept was first discussed by Swiss-American psychiatrist Dr. Elisabeth Kubler-Ross in her 1969 book, *On Death and Dying*.

She wrote that, when facing loss, nearly every person will go through five coping mechanisms, each a different "stage," before they are able to recover. Those five stages are: Denial, Anger, Bargaining, Depression, and Acceptance. Not everyone goes through them in the same order, and some people can hover in one stage or another for a protracted amount of time. Others, still, may circle back through, time and time again, before finally achieving acceptance (Kubler-Ross, 1969). Although often criticized as too rigid a model, this design seems to accurately represent the grieving process for most folks.

It's not within the scope of this book to discuss each of Kubler-Ross's stages, but it needs to be noted that she was the first person to lay out a specific process leading to adaptation. Similarly, the process of adapting to change can be viewed as progressing through distinct stages or phases.

In my mind, I have formulated four.

Stage 1: Resistance. Something is changing, and you don't like it. You may not hate it, but any change requires you to alter your routine. It takes what you know to be true and familiar and throws it into a huge pool of uncertainty. You want to stay in your comfort zone.

Everyone finds comfort with a certain level of predictability. But, with too much predictability comes boredom. Too little predictability, and we feel stress. Change reduces predictability, so our instinct is to fight the impending stress. If someone pushes on your shoulders while you are standing, you could fall. To regain a sense of balance, your body naturally resists the push. Circumstantial change in life creates the same dynamic push and pull.

Stage 2: Complacency. You understand that the change isn't going away, so you force yourself to go with it. You realize that you can't change the change. You still don't have to like it, but you steer into the change rather than away from it. The feeling inside you is mostly ambivalence; you just go through the motions. However, you may feel some frustration. As you enter a new learning curve, you begin to understand the new way of doing things.

Stage 3: Discernment. You begin to recognize the benefit of change. You have been engaged in the new process long enough to notice a positive difference. Your opinion still hasn't been completely swayed, and you do miss some aspects of the old way. But now you are more optimistic about how this "new normal." It may not be so bad after all.

Stage 4: Embracement. Changes implemented deliberately are genuinely done to make things better. After you have mastered the new systems and see the benefit come to fruition, you move forward. You feel no need to resist. You dive completely into the deep end of change because its potential is now a reality for you. The changes have made things better.

At this point, if you do miss the old way of doing things, it is strictly for nostalgic or sentimental reasons. From a pragmatic standpoint, the new way is much better. If you were to do things the old way again, you would favor switching back to the new way.

Change can be complex, so adaptation may go through steps within each phase. For example, a CEO most likely can't predict the totality of benefits and problems of a new technology (for example).

Let's say a restaurant purchases a new POS (Point of Sale) system. The servers used to write every customer order on a pad of paper, hang the slip on a wheel for the cooks to handle in order of arrival, and then manually tabulate the final bill using a calculator and their ink pen, The customer would pay, the server would manually punch it into the cash register, and then the manager would go over the sales totals at the end of the day and separate out all the categories of food, beverage, gratuity, and cash flow.

The new system requires the wait staff to enter the customer's order into an iPad they carry to the table. A touch screen lists the various categories of food and beverage, so once they master item locations, all they do is touch and go. The iPad immediately sends

185

the order to a screen in the kitchen, where the cooks handle the orders as they arrive. When the customer finishes their meal, their bill is automatically tabulated and a sales slip generated. Credit and debit card sales are handled with a simple swipe, and the customer signs the ticket electronically. At the end of the day, the manager gets an itemized report of all the categories of sales and gratuity.

To the owner of the restaurant, this is a perfect solution to dropped sales, mistakes on tickets, coding errors, and phantom transactions where they can't decipher what the server's intention was. Form the servers' standpoint however, this is a complete nightmare! It forces them to do away with the same things they have been doing since Day 1, and requires them to learn a whole new system, warts and all.

During the implementation phase, there is a lot of push-back from the staff. They hate the new system, maybe do a few things wrong on purpose here and there, and are basically bellyaching to the manager about their escalating frustration (Stage 1). After a week or ten days, everyone knows the system in a rudimentary way—but enough that they are functional. They comply with the change, but let the manager know they still don't like it. A few of the "old guard" remind the manager that they are vinyl record albums in a digitized download world (Stage 2).

Then something strange happens—the servers are suddenly aware of the benefit. They don't have to keep track of orders like they used to. If the kitchen screwed up an order (or if it was them!), they know immediately because they have the original order ticket in front of them. And better yet, their tips are always accurate. No more scrounging through MasterCard or Visa receipts to figure out if they were paid properly (Stage 3).

Lastly, the new normal becomes the SOP (Standard Operating Procedure). Everyone has been using the iPads long enough that they are proficient and fast when zipping through an order. The food is prepared more accurately—which makes the customers happy. Happy customers tend to tip batter, so we'll call this a win-win. Oh… and if (God forbid) the system crashes and the servers are forced to go back to the way things used to be, they immediately recognize how the antiquated version of waiting tables is a whole lot worse than they nostalgically remember it to have been.

But here's the part I mentioned about CEOs not ever fully being able to anticipate pros and cons. They know that a change will create an overall good, but there may be some hiccups that require attention along the way.

In our example restaurant, the new POS system works dynamite for regular orders off the dinner menu. However, the managers learn pretty quickly that the entire staff is struggling to communicate special orders or different requests within the framework of the new system. At a staff meeting two weeks after beginning the new iPad system, the servers and cooks come up with an analog way to handle any special requests. The system may not be perfect right from Square 1, but bumps in the road can be managed if the staff remains connected to the management, the business, and their customer base.

***

Perception is a key component of adaptation. A mindset that keenly and objectively interprets situations can efficiently react to change that is otherwise perceived as negative.

Begin with yourself.

The initial impact of being the first to know an important change is about to happen can cause some pushback in your own mind. It's a normal and typical reaction. Many of us have a knee-jerk response that starts with, "Oh, heck no!" It may take a minute or so before it hits, but when it does, let those thoughts happen. Let them pass through you, then let them float off.

The fact that you are the Leader already speaks to the decision you have worked through. You understand the upside value of the change, so any grief over the loss of the "old way of doing things" is far away in your rear-view mirror.

Concern over unknown factors in change is normal for everyone, especially those who lead. But now is not the time to panic. Accept that good Leaders can't fully predict the totality of benefits and problems that come from change.

However, an action plan for adapting to change can help you focus. Obviously, there's no cure-all template for your action plan. Doing the same thing to solve every problem will not work. Each action plan is a unique set of knowable variables, feasible options, and possible outcomes for this particular change. This becomes a thought exercise to help you, the Leader, ease into the change. Those who can evolve and adapt will experience the most satisfaction and the least ambient stress.

As for your employees, you can help them along that path in many creative ways. Remember to maintain that positive outlook and perspective. And true Leaders don't only lead; they guide.

If a recent change occurred that everyone adapted to successfully, use this event to laud their resilience and ability to move forward. Remind them of how well they powered though any problems, and that their commitment to success was very admirable. Positive words can inspire them into a more confident mindset.

If needed, gently remind people that they control their perceptions of an event. This is what their empowerment looks like. The change you are making in your business is neither good nor bad—it's just a change in the way you're doing minor, day-to-day tasks.

Maybe your hesitant employees need the equivalent of the stereotypical joke of how IT tells you to fix your computer—restart it!

With any new hire, the change isn't a change; it's just the way things are done. A new employee isn't aware that a change occurred; they don't perceive any transition from old to new. For them, everything is new, so they adapt immediately.

This may be a way to help current employees have a positive perception of the change. Take your current employees and have them pretend they were just hired today. As you take them through the pretend orientation, ask them what they would think in this situation. Perhaps they may be excited or nervous, but that would be from the usual first-day jitters that everyone gets. In reality, they would have no preconceived notion of how things are supposed to be. They learn how things are in the moment.

Finally, ask them if this new perspective looks a little easier to deal with. Hopefully, the answer will be yes. The hesitant employees can be assured that if you yourself would answer no, you wouldn't have decided to implement the change in the first place!

Training involves more than just showing an employee how to do a new task. Employees need to understand the reasons for the change, as well as how the change benefits them. If the change is profitable, this helps the employees stay employed with the company. Explain that the change will keep the company competitive and afloat; stagnation will sink the business and them, too.

Make sure you and your management communicate the awareness of the immediate struggle this implementation could create. Assure the employees you and the management team will work to help them ease past any obstacles. The employees' difficulty during the transition will not be ignored.

Lastly, keep the feedback loop open between management and staff. Take feedback seriously, as your eyes and ears cannot possibly pick up on everything going on in your company. The folks in the trenches know exactly how the change is affecting them and the customers, too. They can provide critical feedback as to how you might adjust things along the way to smooth the transition.

Finally, the more control employees feel they have over their work, the less stress they will experience. If they know they can voice a concern and it will be taken seriously by their leadership team, they feel more confident in moving forward with your changes.

***

Connection and transparency are crucial when implementing changes that affect employees within your company. Yet, one change has the strongest impact that affects more people than just the employee involved. The time may come when you, as a member of management staff, will need to let the employee go.

Laying off an employee ranks among the most difficult tasks for leaders. Having to lay off staff is very different from the need to outright fire a worker "for cause," as the legal term goes. In this case, an employee who is incompetent, insubordinate, inattentive, or will steal, sexually harass, or physically harm co-workers cannot be tolerated. Managers can make their peace knowing the actions of the employee were the impetus for their dismissal.

In the former case, changes in the business landscape force the company to lay off employees through no fault of their own. I would never minimize how difficult that can be, nor is it within the scope of this book to tell you how to do that. Particularly in smaller companies, that conversation should be extremely personal and very specific to the relationship with the employee.

Changes that are this tough are not made because we we derive joy from it. It is a harrowing reality that has to be done. You get a root canal because you understand the long-term benefits, despite the short term pain and misery! You don't spend money on a casket or an urn because you really love networking at funerals. And, who looks forward to slowly and methodically pulling off an adhesive bandage?

Once again, I bring up my favorite adage: You never know.

Have you ever been dumped by someone, only to connect with an even better person afterward? It's happened to most of us. Getting dumped is never a fun thing to go through but imagine your life if you were still with that person. They obviously neither loved nor respected you, they may have screwed around on you, or they set their sights on someone who wasn't you. How is it better to continue living in a dead end?

You never know what good will come out of a bad situation. For a musician, when a tour ends, we are forced to pick ourselves up, look around for opportunities, meet new people, and make new connections. We never know what will happen next. Sometimes, the opportunity we've been looking for has been waiting for us to be ready for it.

Again, I draw inspiration from the time I screwed up the Rod Stewart audition. I wanted that gig so badly, I had quicksilver in me (as some Italian folks would say). But it was not meant to be. My life opened in a whole new direction when that opportunity went away. As the saying goes: A door closed, but a window opened.

So, I took a hard look at what happened. Would my life have been better if I had toured with Rod Stewart? In the short run, absolutely. It sure would have beat crying alone in my apartment every night.

But how about in the long run? No idea. But I do know this: If I had toured with Rod Stewart, I would have been stuck in a bad marriage and never met my current wife, Shari. I would have never played for Cyndi Lauper or Joan Jett. I wouldn't have become friends with Michael Bolton. I certainly wouldn't have had the privilege of playing with Bo Diddley. All of these opportunities came as dominos falling from the moment I shuffled away from that fateful audition with my head hung low. At that moment, I didn't know what God had in store for me.

So, keep in mind: you never know the plan the universe has for you.

Neither do the employees who are laid off.

When you let that employee go, remind yourself that, from their point of view, this is a kick to the gut that came from nowhere for no good reason. They hurt. And you may feel that nothing you say or do can make them feel any better. You feel their hurt.

As someone who has been there, you also know that this may open a world of potential that person didn't know they had. This event has a strong promise for good.

190

Sometimes you need to get kicked out of your current nest to realize your wings still work.

***

One of the greatest honors of my career was to work with the late Bo Diddley. He was a master of living life by feel. This mindset was so foreign to me, a drummer whose job it is to keep perfect time. I am the total package when it comes to "perfect time," which stands as a metaphor for my life. I do my best to live strategically in a linear fashion. But Bo...man, Bo would read a situation like a golfer reads the wind. He would adjust on the fly and take the rest of us on a wild ride through spectacular music.

Bo was also the kindest, most sincere person I have ever had the pleasure of meeting. He was fun, thoughtful, and always ready to greet you with a smile and handshake.

I played with Bo during the last five years of his Hall-of-Fame life, including his final live show. Looking back, that was a bittersweet milestone. It is symbolic of how fortunate I was to have been with him for a little piece of his life.

I was first introduced to Bo's band through a mutual friend, Jon Paris. Jon is a bad-ass blues-rock guitar player who had invited me to play on a few of his solo blues projects. He ended up getting a gig as

Bo with his drumsticks, ready to play

191

the second guitar player in Bo's band. Deb Hastings played bass and operated as the music director. A woman named Margo Lewis played keyboards in Bo's band and managed him for many years, as well.

Jon called me one night in 2004 and asked if I was interested in sitting in with the band at a jam session in the fabled China Club in New York City. As it turns out, the band was playing at a benefit concert. During benefit events, guest musicians may pop in and play a song or two with the core group. I agreed; it sounded fun. Playing a basic blues number wouldn't be too far of a stretch for me. The night was an absolute blast, and the group raised a respectable amount of money for the charity.

When Bo's drummer moved back to his home outside of the United States, Deb asked me to take over on a full-time basis. We worked out the business end of the deal, and she scheduled me to take over on their next gig at the House of Blues in New Orleans.

I was excited. I love playing at the House of Blues venues. They take good care of their musicians— nearly every detail is attended to. Because I wanted to be prepared and professional, I asked for a CD of the songs Bo likes to play.

Deb's reply was a little confusing. "Oh, yeah...you don't really need that."

Not to be dissuaded, I tried to get a little more information from Deb. I figured I could get my hands on the music if I knew which songs I needed to learn. "How about just a set list?"

"Ah, you don't need that either. Bo doesn't work off a set list. He'll just start playing a tune, and we'll go into it."

Now I was completely thrown for a loop. "Uh, well...would you mind...?"

She gently interrupted me. "Look, Sandy. I'm the music director, but there are some nights when I don't even know which key Bo is going to play in."

She went on to explain to me how she, as Bo's bassist, worked with him. To keep up, she has to look over at Bo's fingering and hand position on his fret board to figure out which key he's playing in. She then gives a hand signal to Margo (*It's in D!*), who then relays the information to the second guitar player.

My brain started silently screaming. Still, I gave it one more shot. Surely Deb could give me something! "I understand, Debbie. Listen, can you do me a favor? Can you at least count the songs off for me so that...?"

She jumped in fast. "No, you won't need that either. You'll get the tempo from Bo. Bo sets the tempo, and you take it from there. You'll be fine."

Okay. Cool. But not really.

I was having the worst trouble ever wrapping my head around Debbie's consultation. It had all the clarity of mud. "Ummm...could we go over some of the potential songs in the sound check?"

"We may not even get a sound check."

After I hung up the phone, I went a little catatonic. What am I going to do with this?

I show up at the House of Blues about an hour before the gig. Up until this point, I had yet to meet Bo Diddley. I was confident with my ability to adjust my playing to match an artist, so I relaxed. I really wasn't that worried about the gig.

With about thirty minutes to go until we hit the stage, Debbie asked if I wanted to meet him. Well, yeah! Of course, I did!

Carefully gathering myself with all the dignity I had in me, I approached Bo Diddley with great reverence and respect. I had been around many high-level musicians before, but this man was truly a living icon of American music. He held out a giant bear paw to shake my hand and spoke with a quiet drawl, "Hey hey! How you doin'? What's your name?"

"Sandy."

"Aww, yeah man. Nice to meet you. You the drummer? We gonna kick ass tonight."

Small talk, but inside me, I was in awe. I had admired Bo for so many years. I felt like a little kid who just found out that Superman was this very real dude who stood right in front of me. It was an out-of-body experience to be standing before him and talking so casually about nothing in particular.

The show went exactly as Deb promised. I sat behind the drums with my sticks in the ready position. Bo greeted the crowd and did his thing while he settled himself on a stool and positioned his hands on his trademark cigar box guitar. A beautiful hush hit the crowd, then his foot started tapping through the anticipation. Instantly, music filled the air.

I had no trouble picking up the beat, just as Deb had told me. Yet, my focus on Bo's tempo was only momentarily broken when I noticed Deb give her hand signal to Margo.

It's in the key of A.

The thrill I experienced performing at that gig was indescribable. Bo brought every ounce of energy he could squeeze out of his soul for the crowd every night, despite how his health would wear him down. His soulful, yet lively, performance was a glowing inspiration.

I played in his band for almost five years, and I grew to really love that man. He would sit around with me and tell stories about Ray Charles, crazy gigs, and just touring the South as a black man in the fifties and sixties. It was an education for me. He reflected on times when he had to use a different bathroom and drink from a different water fountain from his band mates. But if we think that systemic racism like this is only in our past, then we've got a lot more to learn. It never stopped.

***

Bo taught me the value of improvisation, and how spontaneity can lead to magic. We performed a show at the world-famous Paradiso Club in Amsterdam, and that one night spawned most fun I have ever had on stage. It became a seminal moment in my career, compliments of Bo Diddley.

In late 2006, Bo and the band toured Europe. When we touched down in Amsterdam, our first gig was later that same night. It was a long flight, we were dog-tired, and we just found out the airline had lost our luggage. Airport Schiphol is the fifth busiest airport in the world, so I'm sure that the baggage system can be a complicated nightmare. Even so, that was no comfort. Everyone was in a bad mood. I'm serious. I mean everyone was in a bad mood.

We arrived at the venue in the clothes we had worn on the plane. During sound check, the gear they rented for me sounded like dead garbage still in the garbage truck. The mix was off, and the monitor guy was in a lousy mood. He did not want to be bothered. Everyone else in the band had issues with their equipment, as well. The general vibe was like a house on fire, and the only thing available to put it out was a tsunami.

194

Thankfully, about thirty minutes before show time, our luck started changing a little bit for the better. Our luggage arrived, so we were able to get a fresh set of clothes for the performance. I changed into my stage attire, and the change of clothes made me feel more energized. Curious about the crowd, I peeked out from behind the curtain.

The place was packed! Once they threw open the doors, every person in The Netherlands poured into The Paradiso. As they took their seats the air buzzed with anticipation and excitement. When we took the stage, the crowd thew us so much wild energy, it nearly knocked us over! It went into an insane crescendo the moment Bo slammed his foot to the floor in time with a famous blues riff of his.

DUM de DUM de DUM — de DUM DUM

DUM de DUM de DUM — de DUM DUM

At the risk of sounding overly dramatic, the fans absolutely lost their minds. From high atop the drum riser, I could see the entirety of the spectacle. The crowd was jumping in unison, chanting and screaming. My eyes scanned the horizon. From my vantage point, I could see the IJ canal through the windows, alongside the venue. In an unbelievably stark contrast, I gazed at meandering boats parting the canal waters beneath a tangerine sky that cradled the dimming sun, setting down to silently end the day.

Suddenly, it hit me like a ton of wooden shoes: I'm in fuckin' Amsterdam! The entire night was a beautiful dream that could have easily been a scene in a Hans Christian Andersen fairy tale. It was enchanting, incredible, and beyond belief, like a beautiful dream you made sure to remember once you woke up.

As the show ended, we did what we always do. We played Bo off the stage.

I watched Deb closely. She was the musical traffic cop, directing everyone to stay tight and end in unison. There was Bo, doing his thing, waving, and walking off toward the back of the stage. My focus was on keeping his signature beat while he exited.

DUM de DUM de DUM — de DUM DUM

DUM de DUM de DUM — de DUM DUM

Once he was gone, my job was to close the night with five big, accented hits.

DUM DUM DUM— DUM DUM!

The story was told. The end. Or so I thought.

I studied Deb, awaiting my cue for the big finish. The crowd had not lost its energy. European crowds don't cheer randomly or create the deafening white noise that a large American crowd will generate. In Europe, they chant rhythmically. It had the beat of a World Cup soccer final, squeezed into the Paradiso Club.

However, something wasn't right. I kept the beat going.

DUM de DUM de DUM — de DUM DUM

DUM de DUM de DUM — de DUM DUM

And the crowd kept chanting. My eyes remained on Deb, but I was confused as to why the crowd wasn't fading out. Maybe once Bo left the stage, the crowd would fade out the chant, gather their belongings, and head for the exits.

Not this crowd. Their volume remained at a fevered pitch. They were not going to give up and go home.

And then—inexplicably—they got even louder.

I was stunned! I raised my eyebrows so high, they nearly disappeared into my hairline. Still watching Debbie, I think, What the Hell is going on?

She was looking in my direction, but not at me. Her focus shot past me. Something was going on behind the drum riser. Then, the apparition behind me showed itself.

A shadow fell upon my drum set.

Innocently, I looked up, and there was Bo Diddley! He stepped up onto the drum riser. He bent over and dug through my stick bag, grabbing a pair of sticks. When he found a pair to his liking, he turned to me, and his beautiful, wizened face beamed at mine.

I glanced to Debbie, confused as to what to do.

She yelled, "Break it down!"

I immediately knew what to do. I played a quick riff on the drums.

dum de dah de dah — de DUM DUM

I stopped hitting the drums with my hands, but I still kept going with my foot on the bass drum to keep the beat over the frenzied crowd.

Boom — boom — boom — boom

196

A huge grin engulfed Bo's face. He leaned over the drum kit and answered the beat.

dum de dah de dah — de DUM DUM

I don't know how it was possible, but the crowd noise doubled during this exchange. Bo and I fell into a "call and answer" on the drums. I played the rack toms and he answered on the big floor tom. It was 100% improvised from top to bottom. We had never rehearsed any sort of call and answer—heck we had never even talked about it.

I adapted to Bo's instincts. It was synchronized fun! He was a consummate entertainer and always had a natural intuition for what the crowd wanted. Other times, he improvised on stage because he felt like it. Throw it against the wall and see what sticks. And it was always perfect.

From that point on, our call and answer became a nightly ritual. We loved it—and so did the audience. We would change up the beat on some nights completely off the cuff to see what would happen. It never failed to work—Bo had a sense of rhythm and timing that rivaled most all the drummers I knew. He knew how to feel our way through the routine. And it was always egalitarian—he followed my lead, and I followed his.

One night, Bo grabbed me before the show and said, "Hey, Sandy! The sticks you have are kind of thin."

He flexed his enormous hands that could have easily been mistaken for boxing gloves.

He looked back up to me. "Can you get me the biggest, fattest pair of sticks possible?"

I promised I would. I made a call to the manufacturer who sponsored me at the time, and got several pairs of their thickest sticks sent to us.

He tried out the bigger sticks that night and was satisfied with the results. Backstage after the show, he came to me with his brow furrowed. "Hey, man! Those sticks was really cool. Would you mind if I take them home with me tonight?"

I said, "Sure thing, Bo. I don't mind at all."

The next night he approached me, beaming with pride as he held his hands outward. "Look what I did!"

197

Using duct tape, Bo had modified the end of the drumstick to resemble the thick hilt of a sword. Complete with a stirrup looped in a half-circle (or a "guard," if you know fencing), he would pass his fingers through it to secure the stick in case his grip loosened, or he accidentally lost the stick. It was crude and a little visually amusing, but it served as a touching testimony to how important our nightly drumming duet was to Bo.

***

As I progressed with the band, I became the music director for Bo. He called me Red, a nickname that still makes me warmly smile inside. We grew close; about as close as anyone could get to Bo, I suppose. He was a private person in general, but never cold-hearted. He was always congenial and sympathetic.

There was so much heart in everything he played. I wish every musician could have spent time with him to learn how to put emotion into their performance.

I was with Bo when he played his final live performance. We flew in to the airport in Omaha, Nebraska around Mother's Day 2007. Bo had two shows booked at Harrah's Casino in nearby Council Bluffs, Iowa. The casino sent a limo to pick us up and we rode across the bridge to Iowa to settled in for a pair of shows that night.

Between the shows, Bo said he wasn't feeling that good. I asked him what was up.

He paused to think before answering me. "Man...I don't know, Red. There's some brush fires down by my house in Gainesville [Florida]. I've had all my windows open and been inhaling all that smoke."

He looked and acted like his usual self, but still, something with him wasn't quite right.

After we did the second show, he seemed fine. When we arrived back at the hotel, I remember saying goodnight to him in the lobby.

The next morning, the limo arrived to drive us back to the Omaha airport. Bo was a little late to the lobby. I was bothered by this, given his state the night before. As we rode in the car to the airport, Bo became unresponsive. We had no idea what had happened, but we saw that he was out of it. Right when we got to the airport, Margo called 911. EMS rushed to the airport and took him straight to the hospital. Bo had a history of diabetes, so emergency medical attention was an imperative.

I continued on the flight home, not knowing Bo's condition. Later that evening, I learned that he had suffered a stroke and would remain hospitalized for a good while.

Bo Diddley never played a concert again. He only performed once more publicly, improvising a song with musician Jesse Robinson, on November 2, 2007, in his hometown of McComb, MS. He was there to participate in a plaque-unveiling ceremony honoring him on the National Blues Trail.

The band visited him at home in Gainesville, Florida several months later. We jammed a little and encouraged Bo to play along as best he could. He struggled, then let it go. His hands wouldn't receive the signals from his brain. Seeing how frustrated and sad it made him hurts my own heart to this day. It was like he lost his purpose…and possibly his soul.

Ellas McDaniel, aka Bo Diddley, passed away on June 2, 2008. At his funeral, I tucked two drumsticks into his casket. They weren't the sticks with the makeshift duct tape hand guards; I kept those. Mementos of the time I spent with a living legend.

Instead, I tucked two standards sticks in with him. And then I drummed a quiet tribute on the side of the casket.

dum de dah de dah — de DUM DUM

dum de dah de dah — de DUM DUM

I'll never meet a nicer guy, nor one more deserving of respect. Music isn't the same without him.

Chapter 15: Visualize, Internalize, Actualize

Let's bring it all home.

Adjusting successfully to change is the result of being prepared. But how do you prepare for change you cannot predict? The answer: Mental rehearsal. Give yourself the time and space to prepare for whatever obstacle stands in your way. Or imagine you've already adapted to that change, then ask yourself how you got there.

Any eventuality can be conquered through visualizing a positive outcome. Through repetition, this story becomes internalized and put into motion by you and by the higher power that guides you.

I use this exact process myself. I visualize what I want, internalize the concept of success through repetition, and then act to carry out the path I visualized all along. With it, I feel the enthusiasm, as if the outcome already happened.

***

Both Blackjack and Benny Mardones were under the Polygram recording umbrella. By virtue of being involved with these two artists, I became friendly with several A&R guys at the label. A&R stands for Artists and Repertoire. The folks who work in these positions are responsible for scouting new talent, starting their development process, and then becoming the liaison, or the bridge, between the artists and label management.

In September of 1980, my phone rang. It was Jerry Jaffe, an A&R guy from Polygram.

"Hey Sandy. This call is between you and me and the phone. Don't tell anyone you heard this, but Pat Travers is thinking about firing [his drummer] Tommy Aldridge."

That was news to me. He continued.

"I'm not positive about this, so don't hold me to it. But that's the rumor going around the label. Anyway, here is [Travers' manager] David Hemmings' number."

Today, Tommy Aldridge is a good friend of mine. And frankly, I was never a guy who would muscle somebody out of the way for a gig. But I also wasn't a guy who would let an opportunity slip away. So, I called David Hemmings.

"Say, I heard through the grapevine that there might be some turbulence going on with Tommy Aldridge in the band."

He cut me off with lightning speed. "We're not thinking about firing Tommy. You've got some wrong information."

I was disappointed to hear it. But then, without pause, he continued. "If you want to come down to the office, I'd like to meet with you."

He didn't have to ask me twice! I took the cross-town bus to meet David in person.

The conversation was surprisingly relaxing. We sat around and shot the breeze like two old friends. New York people can do that; we fall into a rhythm through our shared experience of the city and all it has to offer.

As I got up to leave, David gave me yet one more covert "read between the lines" moment. He opened his desk drawer and pulled out a cassette tape. "Here's a live tape of the Travers show. All the 'live' beginnings and endings of the songs are there. Take it. You can listen if you want."

I gave him a hearty, "Yes, sir," took that tape home, and learned all the songs on it. No specific audition was held, and no specific instructions were given to me. As far as I knew, Tommy was not being replaced. The transaction was all above board, from David's point of view.

From my point of view, I was now a relief pitcher warming up in the bullpen. I didn't know if the starting pitcher was going to come up with a torn ACL or if he would pitch a complete game. Whatever happened was of no concern to me. I was going to be ready for the game if the manager called upon me.

Back then, I had a day job, but I established a regimen I kept to every night after that meeting. After work, I came home, rehearsed with the metronome for one hour, and then I'd rehearse one song on the Travers tape, over and over, for one full hour. The same song, one song per night, every single night, until I mastered it. I reviewed the first song. I played it through a couple times, knowing I had this one in my back pocket. I moved on to the next song on the Travers tape and played that one for a full hour.

The following night, I reviewed the first two songs and then moved to the third song for a full hour. I did that for two weeks. I rehearsed all fourteen songs on the tape until I had them down pat.

I was very detail-oriented in my approach. One song on the tape was called "Hammerhead," during which Tommy Aldridge performed a solo. The board tape (a live recording made directly from a public address system's mixing console) was recorded in an arena, so there were moments of ambient crowd noise, especially when the crowd went nuts cheering. All that was captured on the tape.

I not only practiced my version of Tommy's solo, but when Pat singled out Tommy ("Ladies and gentlemen—TOMMY ALDRIDGE!") I would stand and wave to the walls of my apartment while the crowd cheered for me. I completely took on the persona of Pat Travers' drummer as I studied his set list.

I visualized myself on stage with the band. I worked myself into a sweat in my apartment. I played every note and visualized/felt success. I can't say enough about the power of visualizing success. It prepares your mind for the triumph you seek.

I was determined to be ready to play if the manager made a call to the bullpen.

I was still practicing and reviewing, until one day I got a call from David Hemmings' secretary.

"Hello, Sandy. Are you available? Pat and David were wondering if you could fly down to Orlando and audition for the band."

Yes I could.

I flew down to Pat's private rehearsal space and auditioned on Tommy Aldridge's drum set for the Pat Travers Band. Pat came in with his bass player, Mars Cowling, who later became my diving partner and lifelong friend.

I told them I knew the whole set. They were skeptical, of course. Who in their right mind would take the time to memorize the whole set list without the promise of ever getting the gig?

The pitcher who wants to impress the manager if he gets called into the game, that's who.

I counted them off, and away we went. We played the first song… second song…and so on. I not only played all the songs, I recounted all of Pat's asides and comments he made to the crowd along the way.

I didn't get the gig right off the bat. Pat knew I could play the songs—I made that clear. What he didn't know was whether or not I would be a good band mate. Would I be a good hang, or would I end up toxic on the tour bus? Did I have a sense of humor, or would I get butt hurt over every little thing? Could I carry on a conversation, or was I going to be a loner who avoided the band?

Not saying Tommy was any of these things, but we all learn quickly that mastering the instrument isn't enough to have longevity in this business. You need to have a personality that fits well with others. Pat hired for culture, not solely for resume or skill, just like any good business owner and executive would.

Pat asked if I could stick around and hang out for a few days. We went to dinner. We hung around the studio. He vetted me for who I was off stage as well as on stage.

After that, he asked if I could stay longer. He wanted to book a couple local gigs so he could see me up and running with the band. I was good with playing in sync with my rhythm section partner, Mars. Pat and David wanted to put the final puzzle piece in place: how well I handled a live gig.

We played the Agora Ballroom in Tampa, then played New Year's Eve at a place called The Button South in Fort Lauderdale. At that second gig, we played the song "Hammerhead." Pat informed me I was going to do the drum solo.

When he announced me ("Ladies and gentlemen—SANDY GENNARO!"), the crowd roared. I stood up and waved, just as I had a dozen times to my apartment walls. This time, it was to a packed house.

Positive visualization. I can't say enough about it. Fill your mind with visions and images of success. Set yourself up to succeed. Had I convinced myself I'd never get the Travers gig, I would have found a way to sabotage my chances. I created a mindset that allowed me to seamlessly step into the role of Pat Travers' drummer. That night at The Button South, it all came true.

I got the gig. We played long after the apple dropped in New York City. Backstage, clinking champagne glasses, Pat made the announcement as only Pat Travers would. He yelled to his road manager, "Hey, Arlo! Get Sandy a tour jacket!"

I couldn't stop smiling. Everyone toasted and applauded. Then Pat said to me, "Welcome to the band, Sandy."

January 1, 1981, I got the Travers gig.

We toured with Rainbow all through early 1981. Later that same year, we recorded an album called Radio Active. In support of that album, we toured with Rainbow, again, as well as Blue Oyster Cult and Heart. Back in the studio, we recorded the Black Pearl album. A short tour after that, the Pat Travers Band was downshifting, and I needed to find another gig.

That took us up to 1983, at which point I met Dave in the Doorway. And that brings us to me joining Cyndi Lauper's band.

Synchronicity, man.

***

When it comes to making a dream come true, always remember the Visualize—Internalize—Actualize model. Commit this to heart as an emotion-backed invocation.

1. Focus on what you want.

2. Visualize as if it has already come true.

3. Take action to reconcile numbers 1 and 2.
   Be enthusiastic about the outcome.

Feel as if you deserve it.

***

A great example of how I accomplished a dream of mine using this method was when I was selected out of the audience by Johnny Carson on The Tonight Show. Before you say, "Yeah, but you're a celebrity," know that this happened before I was even in the band Blackjack. I was a struggling musician that nobody had ever heard of. I was right where you were before you began your career.

I grew up a huge fan of Johnny Carson. One show in particular I loved was the "Stump the Band" segment. Being a budding musician myself, I was enamored by that game. Even after I moved out to California, I fell asleep at night watching The Tonight Show. Over time, I began to visualize what it would be like to be chosen to participate in "Stump the Band." I pictured what it would be like to stare down the unblinking eye of the camera. I pictured Johnny in front of me, wearing a plaid sports coat and holding the mic near my face. I visualized what I would say and knew beyond the shadow of a doubt which song I would choose to "Stump the Band" with. Incidentally, it was a song I wrote, so there would be no possible way they could guess it.

Advantage: Gennaro.

I lived in Hollywood at the time, but Carson was taped in Burbank, about twenty minutes away. In 1978, I tried to get tickets. When I arrived at the studio, I stood in line with everyone else, vying for a chance to be in Johnny's audience.

At one point, an associate producer stepped outside with a bullhorn. He asked the crowd, "We're going to play 'Stump the Band' tonight. Does anybody have a funny song?"

I stepped out of line, hand raised, and joined six or seven other people who had a funny song in mind. We each sang a few lines of our song, a cappella, right there in the parking lot to the associate producer. He picked three of us, brought us into the theater ahead of everyone else, and sat us in specific chairs in the audience. Five minutes before show time, Carson came out and chatted with his producer, who pointed out the three of us who had been vetted for the game.

I had gone over this scenario a hundred times to prepare for this moment—and here it was!

During many of my live performances, I'll show a video of my interaction with Carson. I made it onto The Tonight Show, I chatted with Johnny, I stumped the band, and I got to sing an original song with his band accompanying me.

Johnny was funny, spontaneous, and a perfect gentleman. The experience was everything I expected—and more. I've got to admit, I was nervous when Johnny picked me out and started improvising with me. Even the camera in my face was way more intense than I could have ever anticipated. But the visualization and internalization prepared me for this life-affirming achievement.

You never know when an opportunity will present itself, but if you are prepared and know how to spot it, you can dive right in. Reward always requires risk, but I mustered all the internal fortitude I needed to raise my hand when the producer asked for "Stump the Band" participants. Once I was chosen, I was on my way toward my ultimate destination: an audience with the master of late night!

The takeaway? Life will pass you by if you just sit back and wait for good things to fall into your lap. Define your goals and practice achieving them: Visualize, Internalize, Actualize. Rehearse for the challenge and take the risk.

The universe will come knocking. It's up to you to open the door.

Epilogue

In retrospect, I wonder why I've acted the way I have. I didn't know any of this when I was signing the autograph for Dave in the Doorway. I couldn't articulate these concepts when I said yes to Jerry Renino. I had never written a word when I took a leap of faith and joined Bo Diddley's band.

How did I know to be kind, to just say yes, to help others without expecting a huge return, or to adapt to change? It was a mindset. I acted according to that mindset. I thank my parents for this mindset.

I remember one day when my dad, God rest his soul, said to me, "Don't do or say anything to disgrace the Gennaro name."

In a more positive frame, his message was quite simple: When you act toward other people, make them talk about the Gennaro name in a positive light.

I hope I made you proud, Dad.

References

Alexander, C. (2002). *Breaking the slump: baseball in the depression.* Columbia University Press.

Aristotle, Ross, W. D., & Brown, L. (2009). *Nicomachean ethics.* Oxford University Press.

Chan, J. S.Y., Liu, G., Liang, D., Deng, K., Wu, J., & Yan, J. H. (2018). *Special issue – therapeutic benefits of physical activity for mood: a systematic review on the effects of exercise intensity, duration, and modality.* The Journal of Psychology. doi: 10.1080/00223980.2018.1470487 https://doi.org/10.1080/00223980.2018.1470487

The Editors of Encyclopedia Britannica. (2021). Newton's laws of motion | Definition, Examples, & History. In *Encyclopædia Britannica.* https://www.britannica.com/science/Newtons-laws-of-motion

Gennaro, S. (1985, October). Electronic insights: Approaching the scary monster. *Modern Drummer, 9*(10), pp. 42-43. https://www.moderndrummer.com/wp-content/uploads/2017/06/md72cs.pdf

Hirtz, R. (1999, January/February). Martin Seligman's journey from learned helplessness to learned happiness. *The Pennsylvania Gazette.* The University of Pennsylvania. https://www.upenn.edu/gazette/0199/hirtz.html

Keverne, E. (1996). Primate brain evolution: Genetic and functional considerations. Proceeding of the Royal Society of London, *Series B: Biological Sciences*, 263:1371, pp. 689-696. doi: 10.1098/rspb.1996.0103

Kubler-Ross, E. (1969). *On Death and Dying.* New York: Simon & Schuster.

Lazarsfeld, P. and Merton, R. (1954). Friendship as a social process: A substantive and methodological analysis. *Freedom and Control in Modern Society, 18*, pp. 18-66.

Lorenz, K. (1937). The companion in the environment of birds. *The Auk, 54*:3, pp. 245-273. https://doi.org/10.2307/4078077

McGregor, D. (1960). *The human side of enterprise.* New York: McGraw-Hill.

Megginson, L. (1963). Lessons from Europe for American Business. *Southwestern Social Science Quarterly, 44:*1, pp. 3-13.

Parker, K. & Horowitz, J. M. (2022, March). Majority of workers who quit a job in 2021 cite low pay, no opportunities for advancement, feeling disrespected. Washington, DC: Pew Research Center. https://www.pewresearch.org/fact-tank/2022/03/09/majority-of-workers-who-quit-a-job-in-2021-cite-low-pay-no-opportunities-for-advancement-feeling-disrespected/

Robertson, D. J. (2020, December). Maxims from the Delphic Oracle: Socrates, Stoicism, and the Philosophy of Apollo [Web log post]. *Stoicism—Philosophy as a Way of Life.* https://medium.com/stoicism-philosophy-as-a-way-of-life/maxims-from-the-delphic-oracle-ee2276e7a8db

Schacter, S. (1959). The psychology of affiliation: Experimental studies of the sources of gregariousness. Pao Alto, CA: Stanford University Press.

Seligman, M.(1992). Helplessness: On depression, development, and death. Gordonsville, VA: W. H. Freeman & Co.

Seligman, M. (1993). What you can change…and what you can't. New York: Random House.

Skinner, B.F. (1953). Science and Human Behavior. Oxford, England: Macmillan.

Sports Reference. (2021). *Career leaders & records for wins* [Data file]. https://www.baseball-reference.com/leaders/W_career.shtml

Tope, C. (n.d.). 5 ways to deal with adversity in life. *Live Purposefully Now.* https://livepurposefullynow.com/5-ways-to-deal-with-adversity-in-life/

Wessling, C. (2018, February). Tom Brady named NFL's MVP for third time of career. *Around the NFL.* https://www.nfl.com/news/tom-brady-named-nfl-s-mvp-for-third-time-of-career-0ap3000000913843

Photography Credits

I would like to give thanks to the talented photographers whose work is shown in my book. I apologize to anyone I missed—I have been collecting pictures sent by fans and professionals for over fifty years. I have done my best to credit those who have contributed to this collection.

John Bellissimo (RIP)

Lissa Wales (RIP)

Jules Follett (www.TheSessions.org)

Mark Weiss (www.MarkWeiss.com)

Henry Diltz (www.HenryDiltz.com)

Lynn Goldsmith (www.LynnGoldsmith.com)

Ebet Roberts (www.EbetRoberts.com)

Bobby Levins

Alex Wolff (www.concierge-photography.com/)

Kevin Allen (www.KevinAllenPhoto.com)

Michael van Gelder (photos.GelderlandProdutions.com)

Rick Gould

Chris Helton (www.facebook.com/Christopher.Lee.Helton.Photography)

Rick Malkin (www.facebook.com/Rick.Malkin.Phoography)

Jeff Fasano (www.JeffFasano.com)

Ash Newell

Notes

I am proud to play DW drums, Zildjian cymbals, Remo drumheads, and Hot Sticks.

Suggested Reading:

The Law of Success by Napoleon Hill

Creative Visualization by Shakti Gawain

The Spiritual Laws of Success by Deepak Chopra

Emotional Intelligence 2.0 by Travis Bradbury-Jean Greaves

Made in the USA
Middletown, DE
25 February 2023

25347473R00126